Living
Without Limitations

.

30 STORIES
TO HEAL YOUR WORLD

Compiled by
ANITA SECHESKY

Living Without Limitations – 30 Stories to Heal Your World

CM Publisher
c/o Marketing for Coach, Ltd
Second Floor
6th London Street
W2 1HR London (UK)

www.cm-publisher.com
info@cm-publisher.com

ISBN: 978-0-9928173-2-9

Published in UK, Europe, US and Canada

Book Cover: Csernik Előd

Inside Layout: Csernik Előd

Table of Contents

Legal Disclaimer. 1

Forethought. 3

With Love and Gratitude 5

Introduction 9

CHAPTER 1
The Human Body
By Anita Sechesky. 16

CHAPTER 2
My Healing Journey from Fibromyalgia
By Rebecca David. 22

CHAPTER 3
I am a Caregiver and Healing is my Goal!
By Anita Sechesky. 28

CHAPTER 4
My Heart is the Health of My Wealth
By W.A. Read Knox. 34

CHAPTER 5
How I Found Strength and Beauty from Brokenness
By Kim Thomas 40

CHAPTER 6
Not Limits:
Living Beyond My Wheelchair
By Sujit K. Reddy 46

CHAPTER 7
I Was Finally Wrapped In the Arms Of A Hug
By Sandi Chomyn 52

CHAPTER 8

In the Blink of an Eye: The World I Knew Changed
By Tim Rahija 58

CHAPTER 9

Lifting my Spirit out of the Depths of Despair
By Jill Gjorgjievski 64

CHAPTER 10

**How a Positive Mindset Helped Me Heal
from Neck Cancer**
By Sarah Dickinson Bailey 70

CHAPTER 11

The Human Mind
By Anita Sechesky 76

CHAPTER 12

**I AM a Soul Survivor: Healing From Depression
and Self-Abuse**
By Kaila Janes 82

CHAPTER 13

Yes, I Can Be Sweet as Chocolate
By Anita Sechesky 88

CHAPTER 14

I Was Only Sixteen But I Survived!
By Brian Baulch 94

CHAPTER 15

**I Am The Princess Who Escaped from
the Kidnapping Zone!**
By Monica Kunzekweguta 100

CHAPTER 16

I Have Chosen to Dig Myself Out Of My Diagnosis
By Ronald Goudreault 106

CHAPTER 17

My Relationship was Red Flagged!
By Olive Walters 112

CHAPTER 18
The Power of Unconditional Love Helps Me Transform My Rejections and Inspire My Life
By Viviana Andrew 118

CHAPTER 19
I Broke Through the Wall of Doubt
By Patrick Hayden 124

CHAPTER 20
Woman with a Secret
By La-toya Fagon 130

CHAPTER 21
The Human Spirit
By Anita Sechesky 136

CHAPTER 22
I Always Make Some Lemonade
By Rudo Bingepinge-Dzenga. 142

CHAPTER 23
I Will Never Forget Her Last Words to Me
By Anita Sechesky 148

CHAPTER 24
I Never Got a Chance to Say Goodbye
By Valentina Gjorgievska. 154

CHAPTER 25
The Crossroad to My Healing
By Gloria Delvecchio Callan 160

CHAPTER 26
Death called me BUT my DESTINY answered!
By Janel Simpson 168

CHAPTER 27
Innocence Lost: A Child's Cry in the Dark!
By Kristy-Lea Tritz 174

CHAPTER 28

Healing My Spirit and Broken Wing

By Elizabeth Ann Pennington. 180

CHAPTER 29

I Was Living on the Edge

By Stacey Cargnelutti 186

CHAPTER 30

I Was That Little Girl

By Carol Metz Murray 194

Inspiration comes from our History and Determines
our Future! 199

Afterthought 203

Legal Disclaimer

The information and content contained within this book, "Living Without Limitations – 30 Stories to Heal Your World," is not a substitute for any form of professional counseling such as a Psychologist, Physician, Life Coach, or Counselor. The contents and information provided do not constitute professional or legal advice in any way, shape or form.

Any decisions you make, and the outcomes thereof, are entirely your own doing. Under no circumstances can you hold the Author or "Anita Sechesky – Living Without Limitations" liable for any actions that you take.

You agree not to hold the Author or "Anita Sechesky – Living Without Limitations" liable for any loss or expense incurred by you, as a result of materials, advice, coaching or mentoring offered within.

The information offered in this book is intended to be general information with respect to general life issues. Information is offered in good faith; however you are under no obligation to use this information.

Nothing contained in this book shall be considered legal, financial, or actuarial advice.

These accounts are written based on the co-authors' personal experiences to help bring awareness of health issues, trauma, sexual abuse, harassment, psychological and emotional issues. The authors and compiler assume no liability or responsibility regarding actual events or stories being portrayed.

Information in this book may introduce what a Life Coach, Counselor or Therapist may discuss with you at any given time during scheduled sessions. However, the advice contained herein is not meant to replace the professional roles of a physician or any of these professions.

Forethought

"When we know Love, fear has no value in our presence. There is no
pressure to perform and mask our humanity. We can BE and when we BE,
we can inspire others to BE."

~E'yen A. Gardner

We all go through life hiding parts of our real selves behind masks,
appearing to have it all together, to have perfect lives and to have
no issues or problems. Very few see behind the mask and even
fewer get to know the real you. By hiding our stories, our hurts, our
disappointments, our losses and our pains, we hope people will
accept and love the false image of who we reflect.

As a community leader, church Pastor and Director of an outreach
center, I have spent the last 17 years devoted to helping individuals
from all walks of life find the courage to take off the mask and allow
the light of truth to bring healing and wholeness in areas of emptiness
and brokenness. Witnessing the affluent and underprivileged, the
famous and unknown, young and the elderly all become liberated,
empowered and set free from the wounds of their past has become
my life's mission and my heart's passion.

It's not until we choose to remove the mask and reveal our real inner
truth, in all its convoluted mess and confusion, that our pains and
hurts truly lose their grip on us, and we are launched into our unique
and powerful destinies. The moment we face and expose them in the

3

light of God's unconditional love is the moment we begin the process of liberating every part of our being.

Anita has assembled 25 courageous heroes who have gone through this journey of vulnerably revealing their stories. They have opened their wounds, cleaned them out and have received authentic and lasting change through the victory of healing. As a result they have gone from despair to destiny, pain to power, hurt to hope and trauma to triumph.

I applaud Anita's vision to show the world that they are not alone in their stories; I applaud the inspirational figures behind these stories for bravely removing the masks. I applaud you as you read these stories and hope you are encouraged to take your own personal journey to wholeness. The bible says, "You will know the truth, and the truth will set you free." I pray that you find the truth, and from this day forward you remove your mask and live in freedom.

Pastor Tania Meikle

- Co-Pastor & Co-founder of Kingdom House Christian Centre, Brampton, ON (www.kingdomhouse.com)
- Co-founder & Director of The Impact Centre – Community Outreach Centre, Brampton, ON ((905) 459-5422)
- Honors Bachelor of Science Degree – University of Toronto

With Love and Gratitude

Compiling a book is an adventure. You never know what you will discover along the way. With this compilation, my second major international book project, I had prepared myself and managed to stay calmer and more focused. I did not allow myself to get as emotionally drained as I was after the release on December 12, 2013 of book one, "Living Without Limitations – 30 Mentors to Rock Your World." What a triumph when it became an International Best Seller in less than one day on the market!

Many people may think that writing a book is a piece of cake. I would have to agree with them, especially if it is a single author publication. However in an anthology, what many people fail to realize is that as the main author and compiler you literally have to remove your safety net and step out of your comfort zone. I have had to play the role of consultant, coach, editor, and advisor with approximately 55 people since I started compiling my series of "Living Without Limitations" books. I have come to expect just about anything to happen. As a compiler, your life as you once knew it will become out of balance. In doing an international project of this capacity, you will travel all the time zones in less than 24 hours, many times over. You will have to stretch yourself, expect to have many sleepless nights, and expect very little family or social life. When you finally get to have that long soak in the tub, you know that you have finally accomplished your mission.

That is just a glimpse of what compiling book one, and now book two, was like. You will work with many unique personalities who have many different expectations and you will find yourself either being too nice or too vague. Your goal will only be to make the co-authors look good no matter what they put forth. Your vision has to see beyond theirs and understand how equal collaboration brings balance and fluidity. Many times you won't want to offend, but the greatest reward is that you have successfully managed to single-handedly pull together a group of individuals who have never stepped into the same room. Instead you create a virtual boardroom to manage, organize, edit, and produce a piece of work that, when revealed to the whole world, creates such an incredible shift of perspectives that literally hundreds upon hundreds of lives are systematically touched by the contents within. Many cannot help but be transformed, healed, and altered into meaningful realities that once were lost and bereft of all hope.

To this project I want to offer a generous and compassionate "Thank You" to each and every one of my talented and courageous co-authors who have not only shared their own personal stories, but took my request to be as real and as raw as they could be, to the next level. Their experiences will not only bring tears to your eyes, they will expose your heart and soul to a place that you may never have realized existed in this reality of life as you know it. My desire was for you, our dear reader, to step into these accounts as if you were right there with them. As human beings, we each have a body, mind, and spirit. We are all connected by spirit. We all feel emotions and experience life around us. Let us help you to heal your world, as we have found healing in ours.

I would now like to take this opportunity to acknowledge some very special people in my own world.

To Stephen, the love of my life: Thank you for believing in me and my quest to always accomplish greater things in life. Your love, support and friendship has proven itself through all the trials and hardships we have walked through. Where many have parted ways forever, we realized that the strength of our bond because of the children we brought into this world was greater than the division that life's failures could throw at us. Love heals where words fail. I admire and respect you for your patience, and your determination to always believe that the best is yet to come for us. I look forward to spending the rest of our lives together discovering the blessings that God has for us as a family. I love you.

To Nathaniel: Thank you for being such an amazing son. I love you more and more each day. You make me so proud to be your mother. You are an intelligent, kind, loving and respectful child. I adore your sense of humor and appreciate all the special gifts God has blessed you with. You have an incredible memory and you are very detail oriented, like Mommy. Always remember what an amazing gift from God you are, not only to your family, but also to those around you. Never give up on your dreams. You were a success from the day you were born. I believe in you. Love Mommy.

To Samuel: Thank you, my darling son for the joy that you bring to Mommy. I love your curiosity as a child, always fixing and taking things apart. You have the mind of a genius, and only a mother could appreciate a teapot being turned into a tunnel for little explorers. The world is unfolding before your very eyes. You never cease to amaze me with your growing wisdom and skills. God has great plans for your life. Plans to give you a future of hope and happiness. Success is in every step that you take. I'm so proud to call you "My darling little boy." I believe in you. Love Mommy.

To my beautiful Mother Jean Seergobin: Thank you for always encouraging me to see the beauty in the world around me. To my distinguished Father, Jetty Seergobin: Thank you for showing me that you don't always have to fight to do what's right in life. Mom and Dad: I love you both so much. You have always believed in me even when others have not. Because of you both, I have never given up on the greater good. You each have inspired me to be a better person and look past my own fears, failures and the criticisms of others. I am so blessed to have you as my parents. May God bless you both with long and healthy lives together. I love you Mom and Dad.

To my handsome brother Trevor Seergobin: Thank you for allowing me the room to grow professionally and chase after my dreams, one of them becoming an International Best Selling Author. Your continued support, encouragement and praise make me think of you more as my big brother, but I'm so proud to call you my "Baby Brother." I pray that you will finally find the love that you have been waiting for. Everyone deserves to be loved and appreciated for who they are. You are a success and any woman should be honored to have you in their life. I love you Trevor.

For all of the people who have been part of my life and supported my dreams and ambitions, thank you for being the wonderful friends, colleagues and family that you are. I love and appreciate each and every one of you.

Once again I would like to give an unusual appreciation to those who have caused me heartache, disappointments and pain. Because of you, I never gave up. I forgive.

Introduction

This Book was created based on my BIG vision for the "Living Without Limitations" series with each chapter focused on individual experiences that are centered around finding the balance of mind, body and spirit in order to live a productive and healthy life.

The common thing I kept hearing from my co-authors initially, was how much they agreed we have a world of broken people. They wanted to be part of this life-changing book, sharing their voices to help enable healing on an International level.

It wasn't until after receiving the initial drafts of their chapters that I was able to comprehend the magnitude of healing that was actually taking place among my co-authors and those closest to them. It was then that I realized the title needed to reflect the real purpose based on the concept of my series.

The stories that I have compiled are all "true life" stories. They are neither fiction nor are they embellished to make it a better read. Be warned that they are "Raw," written straight from the hearts of these beautiful souls. When I interviewed each one of my co-authors, I didn't know their histories, or what they had walked through on their journeys to get where they are today. My team and I consist of the most amazing people you can ever meet. We are honest and sincere professionals who have conquered our greatest fears, and now want to help you with yours.

Many times I was shocked and taken aback in tears when reviewing how "gripping" their experiences really were. I found myself asking each collaborator, "Are you sure you want to share this?" The common response was, "Yes! I need to share this, if only to help but one person." WOW! This book had taken on a whole new level that I myself did not expect. You will be introduced to some of the most powerful life stories of what it is like to be "Broken in your Spirit." Be prepared to learn how to find your own healing, when all hope has been stolen, lost or destroyed.

This book is intended to bring awareness of how powerful the human spirit truly is. It doesn't matter where someone comes from; there is still a connection to others elsewhere. It doesn't matter what profession someone specializes in; there is still a connection to all people worldwide. It doesn't matter what age a person is; there is still a connection to all generations. It doesn't matter what gender someone is; there is still a connection between both genders. It doesn't matter what level of education someone has; there is still a connection to those with varying degrees of wisdom and knowledge. And it doesn't matter what religion or faith someone has; there is still a connection to all other faiths. All this can be found and experienced in our beautiful and diverse world, if one truly desires to find it.

This book is meant for you and anyone else who is living with a life experience that may be related to any of the chapters within. It will help open the eyes of those who have never realized how powerful the human spirit really is.

Many times we do not give ourselves, or others, the credit or acknowledgement for what they have endured through hardships, heartaches, pain, trauma or abuse.

My vision for this book is that the reader will enter through the pages and begin a powerful journey that will expose deep layers in one's life. There may be things that you have not spoken of or shared with anyone ever in your life. I encourage you, if you have had, or are going through, any of these experiences or worse, please seek out professional counsel, coaching or guidance from your medical provider, church leader, school official, employer, or otherwise.

Putting your pain aside will only hurt you and your loved ones more in the long run.

If you are like most people, at some point in your life you have to begin an inner journey of healing by releasing the painful memories within your heart and soul. It starts with acknowledgement, forgiveness and then love for the life that you now have. These experiences might be buried so deep that you may not even realize they are still there. Opening up your mind, will and emotions to these stories will allow you to explore the things in your own life that may prove to be therapeutic to where you are right now. Many times we don't realize how our experiences affect every single thing in our decision-making process as we move forward in our journey.

I can honestly say from my last ten years as a Registered Nurse, working closely with individuals in the Health Care field, that I have often wondered about the brokenness that I observed in my patients' eyes. As health professionals, my colleagues and I carry out treatment routines based on physical assessments, medical diagnoses, and information collected or provided by our clients and their families. The main objective is to promote health and healing from a physical, mental or emotional perspective. Unless it is something that requires medicating, many people go through life with broken hearts and spirits that a medical team cannot help with.

Over the years I have witnessed how many people have based their choices on either the things they want to avoid or the things they want more of in their lives. It is a proven fact that we are creatures of habit. If we are comfortable with something, we will continue doing it that way. If we are avoiding things, it can usually be traced back to the negative experiences we had in life.

As a Certified Life Coach, I have helped many people overcome limiting beliefs placed on them by negative and often painful life experiences. Not everyone has the courage or willpower to develop a strong and positive mindset to help themselves overcome and allow healing in their lives.

I will be honest with you. From my own experiences there have been times I had to make some major decisions and was faced with these very thoughts: "What if?" or "Why not?" The "What ifs?" were fear based and always led to one place: I don't want to feel that way again. Therefore my choice was already made for me. The "Why nots?" stemmed from my sense of motivation and courage. I don't know how I found the strength. But one thing was for sure, I was not going to worry about the outcome, because I was too focused on the objective and purpose of my dream or goals at that very moment.

Many times without realizing it, in order to accomplish the things I did, I had to decide to be my own hero no matter what others thought, or how they acted towards me. I am quite aware of the fact that sometimes in life we face circumstances where the difference between accomplishing something of great significance in one's life is deciding at that very moment we are more than what we have experienced or what others thought of us. Not everyone in our lives may be a supporter, motivator, or even healer. There are many people who will not even think twice about discouraging and destroying the hopes, dreams and goals of others. Sadly, it may be based on their issues of jealousy or worse because they have no hope within themselves. If that is so, how can they believe in anyone else?

Broken people will only produce brokenness. They will continue a cycle without realizing they are actively contributing and creating more hurt in the world. This is a natural response which may not even be their own fault; it is what has affected their very souls and only proves that inner healing has not taken place. Perceptions become distorted and narrow. The options in life become very limited because the "safest place" is oftentimes not exposing oneself to the criticism or opinions of others. When an individual is hurt they may begin to start labeling themselves and live in a world they secretly create if they have been victimized or taken advantage of in any way. Evidence of emotional healing is a healthy perspective towards others and your own outlook in life.

There is a connection in the human spirit that I have witnessed in my own life – that no matter what one has faced, forgiveness, love, compassion and empathy can bring healing to many.

YOU may be the very person that needs to have some inner healing take place today. That being said, my desire for you, our dear reader, is that you will choose to be open-minded and compassionate, not judgmental, in a state of offense, or negativity when you read these chapters written with great Love and compassion just for you.

Even though you may have never walked through anything close to what my co-authors and I have endured, as humans we all desire to be loved and accepted for who we are. All of us decided at some point of our journey that there was more to live for in this beautiful world.

When we take a look around, there is so much to be thankful for. Many of you may have walked through worse than we have. Just like you, we all have a dream and together we can walk in hope, peace and unity to bring healing – one person, one soul and one life at a time. We are the hands and feet of God and it's time to replace brokenness, despair and hurt with "Love," the gift of our Creator.

Let's do it! We, as one family of humanity, can heal this world. Let it begin now with you and me.

Anita Sechesky

Anita is a Registered Nurse, Certified Life Coach, International Best Selling Author, Speaker, Trainer, NLP and LOA Wealth Practitioner, as well as Big Vision Consultant. She studied Marketing at the School of Online Business and completed her Advanced Certificate of Life Coaching at Academy of Coaching Cognition. She is the CEO and Owner of Anita Sechesky – Living Without Limitations. Anita has assisted many people breaking through their own limiting beliefs in life and business. She has two International Best Sellers and is compiling her third anthology "Living Without Limitations – 30 Stories to Love Your World," to be released in 2014.

You can contact Anita at the following:

www.anitasechesky.com

🄢 anita.sechesky

✉ asechesky@hotmail.ca

🄕 facebook.com/AnitaSechesky

🄕 facebook.com/asechesky

🄣 @nursie4u

🄟 pinterest.com/anitasechesky

🄛 ca.linkedin.com/pub/anita-sechesky/3b/111/8b9

CHAPTER 1

THE HUMAN BODY
By Anita Sechesky

The human body is the temporary home of the human spirit. It is also the central location where life's actions and reactions take place.

Our body is the most complex and unique life form that has ever existed. Yes, there are other living things, but the human organism is at a pivotal place in comparison to all of the world's creatures. It is a living machine where life is created. Each and every organ is intricately linked together to create a masterpiece of divine workmanship! The systems within our bodies are so detail oriented that even the most skilled engineer cannot duplicate the blueprint to create another human being from the ground up. Each system within our bodies has its own functions and capabilities that, when working synergistically, forms life as we know it.

Like a well-oiled machine, such is the human body when it is taken care of. It can produce so much Joy and happiness by the ability to assimilate responses through the five senses: touch, taste, sight, hearing and smell.

Our greatest accomplishments in life are often attributed to the state of our bodies. When we maintain the function and state of well-being, our bodies will perform at optimal levels. The human body is intricately and wonderfully managed by itself. Yes, it is self-maintained to a certain degree. We, as the owners, must fulfill our role as caretakers and give the proper attention required to regulate it. With proper care, rest and relaxation, it will continue to perform at optimal levels of endurance for longevity.

As we age, our bodies require increased maintenance to continue the activities of daily living. We need to give special attention to ourselves.

Are we receiving enough fresh air, physical activity, rest, relaxation, water and nutrients to stay healthy? We must be encouraged to perform physical activity in order to maintain our full independence free of assistance or ailments. Each of our bodies was created with distinct characteristics, and each takes on its own personality and reactions through its unique DNA. Many people go through their lives not giving a second thought to actually taking care of their bodies. Life can become so busy, and responsibilities get in the way. Eventually before you know, it's the end of another day and no effort has been made. BUT, the great thing about this life is that there's no better time than now to start doing the things you need to do. For instance, when was the last time you did the physical activities you know you should be doing?

Sleep is one of the basic things that is required by everyone, but how much are you actually getting? When you sleep, it is the time that your body effectively communicates within itself. The various organs, the systems and complex cellular activities co-ordinate themselves to promote homeostasis, creating balance within the body, resulting in increased health and well-being. During the day our minds are bombarded by so many activities and responsibilities to attend to.

It is not until we shut down for the night that the body can be completely communicating with our brain, which by this time has begun to sort out all the tasks of the previous day. Goals, setbacks, emotional outbursts and unexpected events are just a few of the memories that must be processed to effectively achieve balance. By the time these are sorted out, the brain begins to have direct communication, giving all its energy and focus to what the maintenance chores are for the body. These include eliminating wastes and toxins, fueling and repairing our cells, as well as processing the communication between the organs and systems. WOW! What a big job! Aren't you proud of yourself? You should be so pleased that you are healthy and on your way to daily healing.

Your mind, body, and spirit are an amazing team that coordinate everything within you to keep you alive! Please take care of it. It is the one body you have for life. Many people unknowingly or knowingly abuse their bodies without realizing the long-term harm or damage they are doing; this also happens due to the natural wear and tear and everyday stresses of life. We can still promote healing within our bodies by making the right choices now. We can begin to listen to what our bodies are trying to tell us. We can connect to the doctors and professionals who know the intricate details of how to help our bodies work even better or help recover the loss from environmental or physical damage. There are many modalities that can be used to help us in this process. But we must be willing to seek out the care and attention with the right resources available.

These are some of the simple ways we can promote healing within our bodies:

- Avoid processed foods, bad fats, and sugar laden items.
- Exercise regularly.
- Get your rest as required.
- Limit your stress load.
- Visit your family doctor regularly for baseline health statuses.
- Research ways you can promote a healthy life for yourself.
- Spend quality time with loved ones.
- Love yourself more; your body knows!
- Do the things that challenge and increase your physical endurance (if you have medical clearance).
- Do not self-medicate.
- Avoid substance abuse of all kinds.
- Take any prescribed meds ordered by your doctor.
- Be aware of your own physical limitations.
- Make informed decisions from reliable sources based on the best outcome always.
- Do your own research and present it to your health provider.
- Take good care of your body. Don't stress it out!
- Don't be an emotional sponge. Let go of everyone else's issues.
- Practice forgiveness and release all of the negative energy.

- Think of your body being at optimal levels of health.
- Associate with others who have a healthy lifestyle.
- Pamper your body once in a while: bubble baths, Jacuzzi, massage, etc.
- Get involved in fun activities that stimulate your senses at the same time: Ballroom Dancing, Belly Dancing, sports.
- Take extra care in what kind of things you feed your body. Does the food you eat promote healing and health?

As a Registered Nurse who has worked in many health care departments with people of all age groups and diverse physical ailments, I am aware that most people, including myself, depend on the health care system. However, my attitude is that individuals should be encouraged to start allowing their bodies the chance to begin healing now, before health issues arise. Give yourself the positive reinforcement your body needs to feel good. The joy and happiness you can create with a positive mindset will get you further ahead in life than you can imagine. Who knows, it might even help to prevent many of life's ailments that can be directly related to stress overload, not only from emotional burdens but also physical demands. We can help to control the load of stress on our own bodies simply by making informed choices when it comes to our food, environment, and relationships. How sad when people are sick or diagnosed with an illness by their doctor that possibly could have been prevented had they sought out the professional counsel and guidance beforehand. I have often observed this in life; because our society is so fast paced, active, and constantly changing, many people don't give themselves the chance to allow their bodies the opportunity to get the rest and relaxation required to bring about basic health and healing. Do you know anyone who fits this picture?

Life is only as complicated as we allow or want it to be. Our bodies are just like any other machine. They will eventually burn out if they don't get the attention and upkeep that they deserve. If you are struggling with negative thoughts towards your health and life in general, ask yourself "Why?" The society that we live in today provides so much information and guidance to help everyone achieve and maintain a standard of health. Seek out the counsel that you require. If you are still unsure what direction to go, discuss this with your health provider.

As you will see within the chapters of this book, many of my co-authors have struggled with their own diagnoses. But they haven't given up. Every BODY deserves the chance to believe in its healing. You know that you are worth it. You are perfectly created in the image of your Creator. Allow yourself the privilege of letting go of all your fears, doubts and heartaches. Nothing is impossible if you honestly believe. If it can happen for others, why can't it for you? After all, you are a valuable person. Everyone that knows you is blessed by the joy that you bring to this world.

Your body is the home that you have been given to live the life that you desire. Don't give up. Live your Life without Limitations. Give yourself the chance you have been waiting for your whole life. With a positive mindset and informed choices, you can begin a healing journey now.

Rebecca David

Rebecca is a certified Life & Health Coach and an International Best-Selling Author in the book "Living Without Limitations – 30 Mentors to Rock Your World," her chapter is titled "Expose And Empower Your Gifts And Talents."

Rebecca's work is dedicated to empowering people to change their unwanted behavior, overcome obstacles, reduce unhealthy stress, and live a healthy vibrant life full of gratitude! Rebecca was born in Southeast Michigan, USA, and currently resides there near her children and grandchildren.

www.rebeccadavid.com

✉ Rebecca@rebeccadavid.com

🅕 facebook.com/rebeccadavidonline

🅣 twitter.com/rebeccadavid

🅛 linkedin.com/sweetspirit

CHAPTER 2

MY HEALING JOURNEY FROM FIBROMYALGIA

By Rebecca David

My path to pursue a career as a holistic life coach came about through my own chronic illness and that of my loved ones; this chapter is about overcoming my own incurable illness of fibromyalgia.

At first I thought I was experiencing some sort of flu or virus, but it was lingering far too long and the symptoms were increasing in duration and intensity. Suddenly I was having a hard time making it up the stairs without gasping for air; just doing laundry was exhausting! Shooting pain appeared throughout my body without warning and in random places! Soon I began to experience horrible headaches due to the intense pain in my neck and upper body. I clearly remember wondering what in the world was going on with me. I also thought I had something wrong with my heart because it was often beating rapidly and irregularly. I had frequent chest pain, intense fatigue and pain everywhere! I had such difficulty breathing at times, especially with any exertion, when I tried to exercise I was unable to move without feeling that my bones were going to break! The intensity of the symptoms varied – sometimes on a daily basis, sometimes weekly – but it was not going away. I cried a lot because I really wanted to do so much and be more active with my family but I was so exhausted and in pain!

After many months of feeling this way I knew it was time to see the doctor. I felt nervous and was thinking it must be very serious to have something suddenly attack my body and disrupt my lifestyle as it was doing! After a full examination and lab work, to my surprise my medical tests were normal, the doctor said everything looked good! I left the visit feeling very confused and with a couple of prescriptions to treat the symptoms.

I sought out several specialists in hopes of receiving answers and solutions, but the only thing I received was a variety of drugs to treat the symptoms; anti-inflammatory, anti-depression, sleeping pills, muscle relaxers, anti-anxiety, etc. The drugs did not heal me nor did they take the pain away; however they did add to the exhaustion, mental fog, and loss of enthusiasm for daily life! It was such a frustrating time to say the least. I was in a lot of pain, but when I took the medications I would often be so very tired or nauseous. Don't get me wrong, I was happy I didn't receive some serious medical diagnosis, but I was baffled how I could be in so much pain, yet it not be evident to the doctors.

A few years passed and the symptoms continued and even progressed. I had been to several doctors and came away from each visit with the same question in my mind, Are You Kidding Me? I felt they didn't take me seriously and that all I was experiencing was not valid to them. I actually considered going to the next doctor appointment wearing some scruffy clothes and without makeup just to appear disheveled in hopes they could somehow actually see the pain I was in and find answers for me! Sounds a little silly I know, but I felt so discouraged to continually hear how good I looked outwardly when I was living with so much pain.

My appointment with a new highly recommended rheumatologist began much like all the other doctor visits, he asked the same questions the other specialists asked. I was getting tired of saying the same story over and over again. After the exam and reviewing my lab tests he said it appeared I had fibromyalgia. He explained that there wasn't a lot known about this syndrome, but it was becoming more common, especially among active women my age. I left the office that day with more prescriptions to take but no hope for a cure.

Well as strange as it may sound, I honestly felt a sense of relief because there was a name for what I had. It was some sort of validation for all I had been experiencing. However, a feeling of hopelessness came over me on hearing there was nothing I could do to heal this pain and fatigue – and that it could very well get worse. Wow, what a range of emotions!

For a brief time I accepted this incurable syndrome and my lot of living with it. Several of my family members also had Fibromyalgia and would say things like "It's in our family genes," or It's our fate." That was very unsettling to me! Many months went by, and I started to feel depressed. This affected me on all levels, because I couldn't find a way to heal it – my daily life and my daily joy were suffering.

After my primary care physician received the report of Fibromyalgia, she spoke with me on the importance of reducing stress in my life and getting good nutrition. I took her advice and began research and implementation of a regimen. There were so many times I felt exhausted but I continued to search out and implement different approaches. I started receiving massages, began journaling, focused much more on good nutrition, researched and used many therapeutic grade essential oils. I nourished my body, mind and spirit with healthy choices and it really paid off! I am so grateful to say that through the holistic protocol I was following the intense pain and constant fatigue began to decrease, and over time it went away completely! I have been functioning at full capacity with zero Fibromyalgia symptoms for many years now; what a difference!

Writing this chapter has brought to memory a difficult time in my life but it is with gratitude that I share this with you to offer hope and encouragement to pursue your own healing, a healing that empowers you and brings about a greater sense of vibrancy in your life. In many ways my healing journey from Fibromyalgia was a gift to me, a gift that allowed me to look at my life in a deeper way. I was carrying a lot of stress emotionally & physically and it manifested in my body.

Dear reader, if you have Fibromyalgia or any other debilitating heath concern and are suffering, in pain and hurting, I encourage you to seek out answers, resources, and tools that will give you optimal health to enjoy life. You will see for yourself the positive changes taking place. It really is possible! There is an epidemic of syndromes and diseases that present with similar symptoms. Many of the traditional methods of treatment cause further problems, like my own increased fatigue, brain fog, upset stomach, etc. We are all different, what works for one may not work for another. There is so much that can be done to ease your daily pain and suffering, and there are a lot of resources available.

True healing takes place holistically, meaning an integrative approach to treating the entire person – body, mind, emotions and spirit. It is a very personal journey; we are each different, and therefore your holistic protocol should be tailored specifically to you.

Here are a few ideas to consider as you begin your healing journey:

- Practice deep breathing frequently. It's a great way to relax, reduce tension, and relieve stress.

- Cultivate awareness. Become more aware of every aspect of your health; choose positive and healthy thoughts and nutrition.

- Improve your nutrition. Eat more fresh vegetables and fruits, avoid processed food as much as possible, increase healthy fats and drink at least half an ounce of water per pound of body weight.

- Research health and healing. There are many free resources on the Internet and at health stores.

- Hire a coach. Working with a holistic life coach can be very valuable; a coach can work in partnership with your physician to assure you are able to live a quality life. If you choose to partner with a coach, choose one who will work with you to create a holistic protocol designed specifically for you. A professionally trained life & health coach will help you process and balance the many emotions you may encounter and will empower you to continue moving forward.

- Embrace the healing journey. When you fully embrace all you are learning and going through, you will begin to understand and appreciate yourself at a much deeper level, providing an even greater opportunity to heal.

With sincerity from my heart, I encourage you to believe there is a healthier way to live, one that eases your pain and provides more energy, I hope you will pursue it diligently. This journey is a never-ending process, for there is always an opportunity to learn and grow. I am so grateful that I am on this healing path and I want to encourage you to begin your own healing journey today. Please don't give up, pursue with diligence your own recovery and healing, it is very much worth it! This is my personal story, I am not a doctor, please seek a health care professional for your health needs.

With much love & gratitude,
Rebecca

Anita Sechesky

Anita is a Registered Nurse, Certified Life Coach, International Best Selling Author, Speaker, Trainer, NLP and LOA Wealth Practitioner, as well as Big Vision Consultant. She studied Marketing at the School of Online Business and completed her Advanced Certificate of Life Coaching at Academy of Coaching Cognition. She is the CEO and Owner of Anita Sechesky – Living Without Limitations. Anita has assisted many people breaking through their own limiting beliefs in life and business. She has two International Best Sellers and is compiling her third anthology "Living Without Limitations – 30 Stories to Love Your World," to be released in 2014.

You can contact Anita at the following:

www.anitasechesky.com

- anita.sechesky
- asechesky@hotmail.ca
- facebook.com/AnitaSechesky
- facebook.com/asechesky
- @nursie4u
- pinterest.com/anitasechesky
- ca.linkedin.com/pub/anita-sechesky/3b/111/8b9

CHAPTER 3

I AM A CAREGIVER AND HEALING IS MY GOAL!

By Anita Sechesky

In 2007 my late aunt was diagnosed with lung cancer. It was devastating news for the entire family. My aunt was my mom's older sister. As a family, we were coming to terms with this news and trying to be as supportive as we could be long distance. During that summer, things got worse. We learned that my mom had also been diagnosed with cancer. My second child was only a few months old. I was on maternity leave from my nursing position at the hospital and was still breastfeeding him, so my days were full as my six-year-old son was now in school full-time.

At this time, we received news that my aunt was given less than six weeks to live. My mom made a very difficult decision to travel from Toronto to Vancouver, and as a family we had to support her. Because mom could not eat solid food she was very weak and got tired easily. Although the flight was long and tedious with the commotion of airport travel, my mom endured it and was determined to see her big sister for the very last time. After we arrived in Vancouver, I made appointments for Mom with a Naturopathologist. She already had a specialist in Toronto, but I wanted her to continue receiving medical care and be free from complications while away from home. Mom received the medical attention she needed while in Vancouver and always said how energized she felt after her treatments. Despite the circumstances I was so happy I could make sure my mom was given the care she required that was available.

The Naturopathologist advised my mom to make an appointment with her doctor right away. It was scheduled when we arrived home and Mom followed through with her appointments.

The reason I am sharing this story is because of the faith that we had to create as a family. This was new territory for us, and we had never walked this path before. We lost my aunt on my mom's birthday, less than a week after we got back home. Even though it was expected, given my aunt's terminal diagnosis, it was still a great loss for us all, since my aunt had been the glue that kept the family together. She always went out of her way to be there for everyone and support their goals in life. Auntie made sure everyone in her family felt important and cared for.

Because my mom's appointments were right around the corner, there wasn't a lot of time to grieve. As her daughter, I realized how much she depended on me to help her stay strong through this whole ordeal. I prepared her meals and literally took care of her around the clock. I had no help, and I still had my young family to look after, so it was a very trying time. What was hurtful was hearing that a few individuals were criticizing me as being irresponsible to my mom because I supported her decision to go to Vancouver to say farewell to her big sister.

One evening we had a visit from a minister. I distinctly remember the conversation getting heated as this individual had the nerve to challenge my mom's belief and faith about healing. I personally believe everyone has the right to form their own opinion when it comes to their life and what their desires are. When someone goes through a crisis, their faith is already being tested and challenged.

We were visiting my mom on the day she was admitted into the hospital; she was scheduled for major surgery the next morning. At that moment in my mom's life, what I observed that she needed was acceptance and support in her faith. This is what fueled her will to survive. I recall there was an unpleasant conversation where I had to speak up. One individual who was visiting my mom in the hospital didn't give a second thought in regards to talking about people who had already died. I was horrified. This was the last thing that needed to be in my mom's memory prior to going "under the knife," thinking about death and dead people. They were ignorant and disrespectful of her feelings and emotions at that moment. Even though I was upset and worried about the impact this would have on my mom, at my dad's request I apologized right away for being so outspoken, even though I felt it was not appropriate. Where were they when it came to my mom's care or best interest all along? I decided that was now their issue whether the apology was accepted or not.

As a nurse, I have great respect for the field of psychology and how the human brain translates conversations, emotions, and their effects upon all the systems of the body. I am a firm believer that positive reinforcement and faith goes a lot further to help promote homeostasis or healing, which can also be called harmony within the cells. Intelligence is a key factor in understanding our diverse and complex biological makeup. When going through a crisis in life, our brain uses all of its memories, emotions, and knowledge to fuel the "will to survive." We become what we feed our mind. My goal for my mom was to maintain a calm and peaceful state of mind going into a surgery where she had to put her complete trust and faith not only in God her Creator and Heavenly Father, but also in the medical team at the hospital in Toronto. I already knew that she was struggling to stay positive for us, her family. But I wanted to make sure that she was not giving up either, especially with this trauma being only two weeks after the loss of her dear sister who was like a mother to her.

On the morning of my mom's surgery, her younger sister, my dad and my brother met me and my husband and our two children at 6 a.m. As a family, we held hands and prayed. The surgeon was Middle-Eastern and respected our prayers. In fact he even allowed me to pray over him and bless his hands. That was a blessing that helped to increase our family's faith.

I learned through my mom's 18-hour surgery, recovery, and six weeks of grueling radiation treatments, that determination and willpower coupled with love for her family and faith brought my little four foot eleven mom through living hell. I have so much admiration and respect for my mom. She is completely cancer free and a living testament to what faith, forgiveness, and loving others despite their negative attitudes can accomplish in one's life.

For those of you walking this journey beside your loved one who may be going through pain and suffering, I want to remind you that the world needs more human angels like yourself. Sometimes the burden seems too great to bear for those we care for. As a care provider, you will endure many long days and nights. There may be times that you feel burnt out and weary. The life that you are used to may be long forgotten. Just remember that your loved one needs you now, and it may be the difference that keeps them from giving up on their own life altogether.

Stay positive! Bring joy wherever you go! Refresh yourself! Whatever you do, know that your love and dedication is not wasted. Indeed, there may be times that you feel unappreciated or rejected. Others may not understand, but at the end of the day, you will have peace knowing that you never gave up and your love and support is exactly what the Great Physician ordered.

For those of you walking your journey alone, either by choice or not, I want you to know that God does love you and that you are not alone. You are important and valuable to everyone around you. Believe that your life has a purpose – and if you haven't found it, what are you waiting for? Don't give up. God has a plan for your life. Do you have one for yours? Every positive action that you take will result in an equal and positive reaction.

What you focus on becomes your reality. Do you want more love? Then give it to others. The simple things we do end up being the most valuable to others. Healing begins within your heart. Learn to love yourself again. Allow others into your world. Seek out support systems in your community, church, school, or place of employment.

As human beings, sickness is not a foreign thing. Unfortunately it may strike at the least convenient times in one's life. Many are not always fortunate to have the love and support of their family and close friends. No one ever said that life was easy. From the day we are born, it is a struggle to survive. We depend on others to clothe us, feed us, and clean us. Then we slowly learn through the following years how to do these things for ourselves. Our lifecycles revolve from being dependent to independent and then if sickness strikes before aging, we become dependent on others all over again. One thing is sure, we've all been given this one chance to make the best of this life we have.

Living *Without* Limitations

W. A. Read Knox

W. A. Read Knox is an International Best Selling Author and Certified Life Coach living in Hunt Valley, Maryland, USA. He is the father of five children and has one grandchild.

Read is a Realtor and has experience in numerous businesses over the years involving Aviation, Trucking, Mortgage Banking, Natural Health, Professional Sports, Frozen Foods, and licensed Life and Health Insurance and Investment Broker. Read is an avid athlete with a passion for Squash, Tennis, Skiing, Motorcycling, Polo, Hockey, Sailing and Travel. Interested in ReDox Science and its ability to change our health through Bio supplementation. He wrote the chapter, "Break The Blocks to Business Success!" as a co-author of "Living Without Limitations – 30 Mentors to Rock your World," also compiled by Anita Sechesky.

www.awesomecells.teamasea.com

www.readknox.fgxpress.com

www.readknok.nerium.com

www.awesomewater.info

✉ Readknox@gmail.com

⬤ facebook.com/read.knox

CHAPTER 4

MY HEART IS THE HEALTH OF MY WEALTH

By W.A. Read Knox

The tower controller at Martin State Airport, in Baltimore, Maryland ordered, "You are cleared to land Mooney November Two Two Two Eight Kilo (N2228K), Instrument ILS approach runway 15 and watch for traffic... should be Medevac State Police Trooper Two leaving from the Helipad." My instructor told me that we were going to keep practicing these instrument-only approaches all day until I could hit the landing threshold every time! Flying was so much fun and such a challenge for me, and I miss it every day. I had the best flight instructor – who even flew with me from the east coast to the west coast just for the fun and the experience!

Flying saved my life and almost took it several times over the years. Let me explain how flying saved my life. Every so often your pilot's license needs to be renewed. Well it is the medical examination part of the process that took away my license to fly.

I went to the Aero Medical Examination appointment with expectations of breezing right through, as I was in great shape and running five miles a day. However, the doctor looked up from listening to my heart and said, "Did your doctor ever tell you that you have a heart murmur? You need to see a cardiologist before I can clear you to fly again!"

Those words would be echoing in my ears all week, as I waited to see my friend and fellow squash player and now my cardiologist. He first listened to my heart and then sent me across the hall to have an echocardiogram. The operator of the machine which was imaging my heart and measuring all aspects of each beat says, "Son you have the heart of an eighty five year old man. There is a huge calcium deposit in your aortic valve, and you will need surgery. (I was a healthy middle aged man, I thought.) I am not supposed to tell you any of this so act surprised when the doctor tells you!"

The doctor told me I would in fact need surgery, and I almost passed out in his office. I had never had that feeling of disbelief, raw fear, and dread before in my life. I then heard him ask me if I wanted a dead person's valve, a cow valve, pig valve, or mechanical valve? I clearly had some homework to do and many more medical tests, and I managed to put off my surgery for several years as my condition, a bicuspid aortic valve with a large aneurysm, was closely monitored for changes. As the aortic aneurysm reached the critical threshold in size where surgical intervention is recommended, I was forced to decide what kind of valve I would get, and I chose an On-X with New Mechanical Aortic Heart Valve which was very new at the time and not recommended by my cardiologist or surgeon. The implantation of my valve was to be the second one implanted at the hospital by a world renowned surgeon and his amazing team.

The process of preparing for a life threatening surgery is different for everyone, but for me the thought of dying or being crippled from the surgery was so scary and I felt just fine the way I was. I was thinking, "Why am I deciding to do this to myself? Am I making the right choice with a mechanical valve? Is this the right doctor? Is this the right hospital?" Suffice it to say that a million questions went through my head every day, until I found myself saying goodbye to my wonderful wife and five children. Then I was wheeled into the operating room to have my life change forever. I remember very little about what happened next, but when I regained consciousness I was strapped down on a gurney with a tube down my throat and a mechanical respirator breathing for me.

I remember I could see a clock and it was ticking; I remember the nurse telling me to be still and stop thrashing and fighting the machines that were keeping me alive. I heard the doctors and nurses running down a checklist of items, kind of like one I would go through before flying my plane – only this one was used to save a person's life. The patient in the bed next to mine was crashing and they re-opened her and were trying everything they could to save her, but she died. I then remember being moved to a new location and listening to the nurses arguing with each other as they wheeled me and my machines to another location.

When I finally had the tube removed from my throat, I was so happy to be alive and really wanted a sip of water or an ice chip! To my surprise, I was too weak to even lift a paper cup. That was how much this surgery had taken out of me. I had just survived the procedure of "total circulatory arrest," where my body was cooled to about 64°F by a heart lung machine, and my head and chest and body were packed in ice. My heart was stopped, lungs deflated and all the blood was drained from my body into the heart lung machine. I was clinically dead. The heart lung machine was turned back on after the surgeon finished replacing my aortic root with a Dacron graft and the On-X with New Mechanical Aortic Heart Valve and reattached the major arteries to the graft. A patient can survive in this state for about forty minutes before the process damages the brain, heart, or the lungs. My entire procedure was somewhere around eight hours long and I was one of the luckiest people in the world that day, and it was Friday the 13th of June, 2008.

I remained in the cardiac intensive care unit for the next seven days, waiting as patiently as I could to get a permanent pacemaker implanted. I had wires and tubes coming out of everywhere, and a temporary pacemaker that was run by replaceable batteries was sitting in my lap keeping me alive. Every so often my cardiologist would come in and turn it off to see whether my heart would beat on its own again. I would just about lose consciousness each time; it was like being in Oz. Sometimes the electrical pathway of the heart is damaged in the surgery, and the bottom of the heart doesn't get the electrical message from the top of the heart that it is time to beat. I gradually had to accept that I was in the "1% of people" that this happens to. At least this was a complication that could be fixed. I now am kept alive by a small computer implanted below my collarbone and I am a grateful walking miracle of modern medicine.

"YOUR HEALTH REALLY IS YOUR WEALTH"

Without your health it really doesn't matter how much money you have, what your job is, where you live, or anything else like that. When I faced a surgery of this magnitude, looking death in the face, what mattered the most to me in my life was my family. My amazing wife, my mother, my four daughters, and my son were there to help take care of me at the hospital and during my recovery at home. My brothers and sister were there for me on the phone as well. If anyone out there reading this has any doubt about how amazing and wonderful this was, let me assure you that having my family care enough about me to be there for me when I really needed help was the greatest gift I have received in my lifetime. I am truly the most grateful person for the gifts of love and family that have been bestowed on me.

For anyone that is going through any heart disease and needs to have a heart surgery believe me that I get that "THIS IS GOING TO BE JUST A ROUTINE PROCEDURE" is something we all hear from our doctors and our friends and family. Believe me when I tell you that it doesn't feel that way when it is YOU who is going on the operating table. Now that I have recovered, I can tell you that I have never felt better than today, having just survived past the critical five year anniversary of my surgery. Although I am no longer a private pilot there are many other fun things that I can do every day, especially being a father.

There is hope and health beyond the surgery, but courage and valor and fear and death are in between...and LOVE is what cured me! That is just a small part of my story, May God Bless You Too!! I encourage anyone that can relate to my story, or if you would like to work with me around any fears you may have and how it is affecting your business or life, I am a Professional Life and Business Coach and am available at the above links.

Kim Thomas

Kim Thomas is on a mission to inspire others to pursue their passion and transform their lives from broken places to fulfillment and purpose. Kim is a Certified Life Coach, Health & Wellness Consultant, Motivational Speaker, and CEO of onLIFESTYLEwithkim.

With over 20 years of experience in education as Teacher and Success Coach, Kim has an extensive background in the Arts – as Creative Director, Actor, Writer and Producer. Her commitment to creating an enduring legacy is only surpassed by her passion for family and her three remarkable children, who inspire her to pursue greatness and make a difference in the world.

www.Onlifestylewithkim.com

✉ Kimnthomas@gmail.com

f Kim Thomas

🐦 @Kimeika

📷 Kimnthomas

CHAPTER 5

HOW I FOUND STRENGTH AND BEAUTY FROM BROKENNESS

By Kim Thomas

I would have never anticipated my fate on that sunny and crisp fall day on October 19, 1987 – also known as Black Monday – when stock markets around the world crashed. Well not only did the financial markets crash that day, but so did the vehicle I was driving in on my way to the dentist with my younger brother. I was 17 at the time, and while that seems like a lifetime ago, it is very clear to me that the lessons I learned from that near-fatal car accident would set in motion many things that would help shape my life today. It fueled my lifelong passion to help others realize that there is something greater inside us that enables us to overcome every adversity, and that strength, beauty and courage truly come from within.

My car had been hit by an erratic driver who was going over 100 mph, blazing through the red light and hitting my car broadside, sending it airborne. The car was crushed and witnesses couldn't believe we were still alive. Thankfully, my brother hadn't sustained any life-threatening injuries – but even today those gripping moments that we shared still give us an unshakable bond.

The first to arrive at the hospital was my mother. Doctors warned her, "Your daughter's entire body has been badly broken." But their dismal report did not intimidate her; instead she fought fear with prayer and unshakeable faith. My brokenness extended far beyond my physical trauma. Inside I felt helpless. I saw my future flash before me; every dream faded as I lay there with many questions of whether I would ever walk, see, or even look the same again. I had many head injuries including a fractured skull, a detached eye, shattered facial bones, deep lacerations on my face, a broken collar bone and a shattered humerus. And over 70% percent of my blood was depleted, causing the most imminent fear of death.

At 17, I didn't understand that God would allow us to become broken in order to build us up. The doctor who performed the eye surgery warned my parents that while he was able to re-attach my eye, it was unlikely that it would function normally again. Another doctor warned that while I would walk again, there were no guarantees that I would have full mobility. The plastic surgeon said he could eventually bring my face back, but couldn't guarantee what normal would look like. What a dismal report, but thank God for my close-knit family. My mom, dad and three brothers rallied by my side to speak words of life. My brother, who is now a Pastor, read Psalm 23 to me every day. Yet I still struggled with the feeling of despair. I couldn't see past my present circumstance and couldn't help but feel bitter because I should be at school training for track & field, rehearsing for the school play, getting ready for Grad photos or getting glammed up to attend Prom like everyone else. I just wanted to enjoy the things that typical teenagers do. Instead I was worrying about what my future would look like.

There were days when I felt like I was at my own funeral; visitors often looked mortified when they came to visit. One of my friends even threw a vase of flowers at the window in a rage, sending shattered glass everywhere, prompting nurses and security to rush to this scene of fury. Because my face was stitched and wrapped shut, I wasn't able to comfort my friends and reassure them that I would be alright, but truth be told, I myself wasn't convinced that I was going to be alright. After several angry and loud visits, security was posted outside of my room and eventually my elderly roommate requested to be moved – the mayhem was becoming too much for her.

The next morning, I asked the nurse if she could wheel myself over to the washroom so I could see myself in the mirror. Strangely, she said that strict orders had been given that I wasn't to see myself, because I was on suicide watch. Did they really think I would kill myself? Now I was really curious about what I looked like, so the next day I asked my mom to bring in a hand mirror, so I could finally look at myself. With no hesitation my mom said, "Of course I'll let you see yourself, because one day you will look more beautiful than ever." In that still and quiet moment, my mom placed the mirror in front of my face with such confidence, but to my greatest fear, what I saw was more horrific than I ever imagined.

Part of my hair shaved off, the rest still knotted together with blood, a disfigured nose, a bruised and stitched up face, and even worse, my face was so big and swollen that it couldn't even fit in the mirror! In that moment I was so angry with my mom for even suggesting that one day I would look better. Overcome by despair, I asked God why He hadn't just allowed me to die. I realize that people go through tragic circumstances all the time, but no one ever expects that tragedy will knock on their door.

After feeling that I had hit rock bottom emotionally, I decided that I was going to fight the good fight with faith. I pulled on something that was greater than me. The Words of hope and healing began to manifest not only in my mind and spirit, but also in my physical body. Though still weak, I began to feel strong. I soon realized that no matter how much someone prays for you, ultimately, you have to believe it for yourself. You have to trust that all things are possible, and that when you have no words at all, simply having faith the size of a mustard seed is enough to move mountains.

I quickly realized that God was on my side and was waiting for me to unleash that giant called faith that He deposits in all of us, but which only we have the power to activate. Although I was in a lot of pain, looked horrific and was uncertain of my future, I was grateful to be alive and realized that He that is within me, is greater than any circumstance. I said, "Lord use me to transform other lives through this experience." At that moment, I could hear God audibly say, "I saved you because I have great plans for you. Do not fear because I will take care of you and give you a future and a hope."

Fast forward to several months later, I began to see miracle after miracle in my life. Doctors were blown away. Even though I experienced much transformation, it took some time before I really felt and looked normal. I often fought back tears and faked confidence, yet I could hear a still small voice reminding me, "When you are weak, I will make you strong." I moved forward, knowing that my destiny and calling were greater than my insecurity.

Two years after the accident, I was miraculously healed and didn't even require the plastic surgery that was scheduled for me. They say everything happens for a reason, and I totally believe that. This trial has allowed me to speak to countless people over the years, especially girls that struggle with low self-worth. It birthed my mantra that strength and beauty come from within, and that we are born to make a difference. It is time to see every test as a triumph, every battle as a blessing, and every opposition as an opportunity.

Our life has purpose. One that we often ignore and don't fully walk in. Let your difficulties fuel your faith and become opportunities for God to catapult you to higher heights – so when you rise from the valley to the mountaintop, you have greater vision, passion and purpose. Know that every adversity you face is opportunity for God to unleash His power.

You only know how strong you are when you are faced with a battle, but there is something greater inside of you that builds character, perseverance and compassion. There's redemption lying deep within that brokenness. Make room for God and allow yourself to embrace every struggle and circumstance, because there's purpose on the other side of that pain.

Through life's experiences, you quickly learn that when you have nothing but faith, that's all that you need. When adversity comes your way, don't take it personally, take it spiritually. The mantle of greatness doesn't come easy. We all have to fight through battles to get there, but God beckons to us to be still and know that He is God. Find hope in the detours that life brings, because your miracle is someone else's miracle. Believe, trust and have faith like your life depends on it.

Sujit K. Reddy

Sujit K. Reddy excels at everything his sets his mind to do. He is a seasoned HR Professional who has had more than a decade of experience in influential roles. Such roles include working with three Canadian Financial Institutions (i.e., RBC, TD, and Scotiabank). He runs his own HR consulting firm. He assists people in attaining their ideal lives through a growing international movement. He speaks on various topics using life experiences for all types of audiences. Sujit enjoys spending his free time travelling locally and internationally. Throughout his life Sujit has sought to make the world a better place for all.

www.humancapitalsolutions.co

✉ info@humancapitalsolutions.co

⬤ facebook.com/THESujitK.Reddy

⬤ twitter.com/Sujit_K_Reddy

⬤ linkedin.com/in/sujitkreddy

CHAPTER 6

NOT LIMITS:
LIVING BEYOND MY WHEELCHAIR
By Sujit K. Reddy

Let me start from the beginning so that you get a clear sense of who I am and where I have come from. I was born on February 25, 1977, in Toronto, Canada. I was the first-born of two loving immigrant parents from India. I have two loving younger sisters.

I was born with spina bifida and hydrocephalus. Being born with the medical diagnosis of spina bifida meant my spine was deformed at birth, and as a result I am not able to stand or walk, nor will I ever in my life. So, to move about, I use a manual wheelchair. The medical diagnosis of hydrocephalus at birth meant I was born with too much water on the brain. This excess water was drained in an emergency surgery, by way of implanting a shunt which is a long thin tube that unraveled inside of me as I grew. The shunt starts at the back of my head and drains into my abdomen. Fortunately, this shunt has never been a serious medical concern in my life. As a side effect, I do have a few slight learning disabilities to do with math and writing; but over the years, I have figured out ways to manage them.

I have had many struggles, trials and tribulations throughout my life, as we all do. I was not raised by my parents to use my physical challenges and the few limitations that come with them to have people feel bad for me, take pity on me, or most importantly, feel sorry for me. I was raised by my parents to be an equal in my family and the world. I have two younger sisters, and growing up, if they were rewarded for something good they did, I was rewarded in the same manner. On the other hand, if they were scolded for something bad they did, I was scolded for the same thing, in the same way.

My parents instilled in me that I must show the world that, although I am in a wheelchair, I am able to live beyond it. In other words to focus on the positives in everything that life hands you. Even my given birth name 'Sujith(sp?) Kumar' is a constant reminder of this, as it translates from Sanskrit to English to mean "Victorious Prince," which I have always taken to mean that I should never give up, no matter what!

I feel it is important to make specific mention of my father. He passed away when I was just seventeen. My father was not only my father, but my best friend and first mentor. He taught me how to live and be independent. Looking back on the time that I did have with him, I have come to realize that he taught me – both directly and indirectly – everything I needed to know in life.

I will give you some examples to illustrate this. Both will come from the numerous family vacations we took together. My father directly taught me how to manage in any situation and in any surroundings. For instance, there would always be a different setup in terms of washroom facilities, whether it was in the hotel room or if we were staying with relatives or friends. My father taught me to adapt and change based on what was available to me in each case and not to focus on what was not. Indirectly, my father taught me how to deal with people's reactions to me and who I am as a human being. Whether it was looks, stares, glares or comments, my father taught me how to react in a positive manner to such negativity.

As a result of my childhood travel experiences, I have always enjoyed traveling to various destinations in the world as an adult. Such places have included various states of the United States of America and various countries in Europe and Asia. Throughout my travels outside North America, I have noticed one theme. That is, people with disabilities aren't always treated as equals by their respective families, communities and societies. What I have observed is that people with disabilities are often "forgotten" and "put aside." Infrastructure and attitudes are not supportive to allow a person with any form of disability to live freely and independently as it is in North America for the most part. Every time I have traveled, I feel so blessed for the life I have had and have, and the opportunities I have been afforded living in Canada.

I have traveled to India numerous times, as the majority of my extended family resides there. For those of you who have not been there, India is not known to be the most accommodating or accessible country in the world. I must say though, in the past twenty years, India has made some effort towards being more "livable" for all persons with disabilities. This is mostly due to foreign investment; but it still has a long way to go as a nation to equal the standard of living that people with disabilities experience in North America. I will give you an example from a sightseeing tour of Northern India that I took with my family and cousin.

One of the main stops on the tour was the world renowned Taj Mahal in Agra, India. This was something on my "Live List" that I had always wanted to do. It has been declared a "historic" site. As a result, no accommodations have been made to make it accessible. If you have ever had the opportunity to visit the Taj Mahal, you will know that the stairs, to get up into the main court yard, are steep and narrow. I took one look at the gentleman who was "assigned" by the tourist administration, to "help" me up the stairs, and knew I was going to be in some serious trouble if I were to get him to assist me. He was a frail man, in his 60s at best! He and his colleagues were suggesting it was too dangerous to get me up the stairs. I looked at my mom, sisters and cousin and they instinctively knew what was coming. I climbed out of my wheelchair, and pulled myself up the stairs on my own! I then had my sisters and cousin bring up my wheelchair behind me so I could use it around the grounds. There was no way, after travelling all that way that any one was going to keep me from seeing this great Wonder of the World!

It is my hope that something I have said resonates with you, and I have moved you positively towards attaining your goals and dreams. I hope you have found something in what you have just read, to be and do better in your lives and fill the world with positivity, and let it shine and flow to those around you and even beyond that, to the entire world.

My entire life, I have always wanted to prove to the world that being a person born with a disability and in a wheelchair does not mean that life has to be limiting. I have made my life fulfilling and continue to do so every day.

As a result of the motivation and focus my parents have gifted me with, I have accomplished more in my thirty-six years than most "able-bodied" persons have and do in that same period of time.

Many parents of children with disabilities allow their child to coast through life and "take it easy," not allowing them to apply themselves, to change the world for the better. My parents never allowed for this to take place, and I am so thankful for that now because I am truly living life to its fullest, with a feeling of joy and abundance.

I have lived independently for over a decade now, with some assistance of government-funded attendant care (i.e., cooking, housekeeping, laundry) and have a decent and very active social life. You too can have the life you desire if you focus on the positives in your life!

"You can accomplish anything you put your mind to. Your mind ONLY has the limitations that you allow it to have.

Every person, regardless of the unique characteristics that make them who they are as an individual person, has the right to live their life without limitations.

Do not let diagnoses or disabilities limit your potential as a human being. You were created for a purpose. Think BIGGER. Think past the confines of your limitations. Let healing begin within your life. Let go of all the labels and listen to your heart. Everyone can make a difference, one person at a time. Be courteous and respectful. Everyone deserves respect.

"Look around you and see what others like you have already accomplished, and strive to do better."

~Anita Sechesky, RN, LC

Sandi Chomyn

Sandi Chomyn is a life coach known as a Life Management Coach. After raising her three boys, she received her coaching training with Coaching Cognition. She's a farm mom and grandma, inside and out, and has come to enjoy the different facets of her life by integrating her life coaching business and her love for scenic photography with good country living. She's also an International Best Selling Author with a chapter called "In Search of True Happiness" in the book "Living Without Limitations – 30 Mentors to Rock Your World." She resides with her husband Bill in a small farming community in Togo, Saskatchewan Canada.

www.sandichomyn.com

facebook.com/meetsandichomyn

facebook.com/sandichomyn

sandi_chomyn

pinterest.com/sandichomyn

Sandi Chomyn

CHAPTER 7

I WAS FINALLY WRAPPED IN THE ARMS OF A HUG

By Sandi Chomyn

I was in a foster home from the time I was an infant. Looking back, there was a mixture of good and bad experiences.

Up to the age of seven I did not realize or know I was in foster care, until I was told I was moving to a new home and new people that would be looking after me. It was just me moving on, nobody else. Suddenly, I had the sense of uncertainty and confusion. I felt very scared and alone for the first time in my life. It made me think I had done them wrong and they did not want me anymore. I was the bad child.

This new foster mom showed me all of the things she thought and felt I needed to know about household chores. I learned about cleaning, cooking, laundry, and gardening and was given an education. She told me these were things I needed to know when I was older and would be on my own in the world. I was there until I got married. At the time it was an escape to get away, as I felt I couldn't make it on my own.

As long as I can remember from an early age, things were always very impersonal in both foster homes. Not knowing any different at the time, I thought it was normal. Even though I saw things were different in other people's lives, I did not question it.

At a young age did I realize I was learning about different emotions? In my own way I most likely did but did not recognize them the same as others may have or should have or could have. My classmates called me retarded and teased me about being a foster child. I was always told by my foster parents and teachers that I would not amount to much of anything, because in their eyes they assumed I did not care or was a difficult child and student. In response I felt like nobody cared about me. I felt I was never good enough in their eyes. I was doing, so I thought, all of the right things or the things they were teaching me to do, but I still felt that they were judging me. Even though I had done everything that I was supposed to do and was told to do. This made it more difficult for me to understand what was going on in my life. This in turn made me defiant as I felt that is what they wanted.

As I was getting older, I was starting to recognize things within myself with mixed feelings. There were many emotions I had that totally confused me. I started comparing myself to others and noticed that I was "different," and my perception of what I felt was normal was starting to make me ask questions. But the questions were only in my own mind, as I felt I should not or could not talk about it. And in reality, at the time, I felt I had no one to turn to.

It was important to know what was happening in my life. I needed and wanted someone to explain the situation to me in a way that I could understand, someone I could trust and talk to about things. But I never had that, and then just pulled away in many ways.

In my late teens I was assigned a new social worker. When she came for scheduled visits, she took time with me. Suddenly, my opinions were important to someone. There were times she even asked me for advice. It was the very first time in my life that anyone seemed interested in me and my opinion. It helped me to start feeling confident in myself and to see that I had important things to share. She understood my needs, abilities and capabilities. We worked together on my school work, and together we built up my self-esteem. I started to be proud of who I was and know I was a beautiful person. The relationship with my social worker provided me with stability and helped me to feel less afraid. I didn't change overnight. It was and still is an ongoing growth. Now I love to communicate and share advice as a life coach. Maybe that social worker is reading this right now. I would like to say thank you as I did not get a chance back then. She had moved on to new things in her life.

My biggest turning point was a lesson learned from my fiancé's mother. I had gone to the city with my future husband to go shopping and to the summer fair for the day. We then went over to his parents' for the evening meal and for a visit. As we were getting ready to leave and chatting at the door my fiancé's mom reached out and gave him a big hug. As I was standing there waiting to go she turned to me and enveloped me in a big hug that had me in shock. I had never been hugged like that before. I stood there not knowing how to act or feel about it. Yes I had had boyfriend hugs but never a hug from anyone else.

My fiancé's mom felt there was something missing when I didn't return the hug the same way she had given it. She looked at her son and asked what was wrong in her native tongue. Her son wasn't sure what to say. They both looked at me for an answer, which I wasn't sure I could give them.

Without saying much as it was an awkward situation, we let it go. I didn't though. I did a lot of thinking about it the next few days and weeks. I had a lot of mixed feelings about it because I wasn't someone who would talk about it, I internally processed it.

Days and weeks passed and I was to visit my fiancé's parents again. I still felt intimidated and unsure. We had our visit and were getting ready to go. Standing at the door my fiancé's parents gave him his hugs and "I love you." I was standing there waiting. When they were done; instead of them reaching out to me, I reached out and gave both of his parents a hug. I thanked my fiancé's mother for teaching me something special that day of the fair. I then explained to them that I didn't receive hugs growing up, and that it was something new for me. She asked me why I had never been hugged. I told her what I only knew. I mentioned that I was a foster child and that they never showed the emotion to me like they did to their own children. Saying to her, somehow in my mind I thought it was normal but down deep knew it wasn't normal to even think the way I did. She said, "That was so wrong." We talked more about it through the years. For opening up to her I was wrapped in the arms of a hug by my fiancé's mother. This was the start of many more hugs and "I love yous" to come.

My fiancé, at the time, also taught me someone did care about me and that I was more than good enough in their eyes. He always told me I am capable of doing anything I want and being the person I want to be. Through his love and understanding and not judging me, I have become that person. I have taught my own children that these two things are very important. They do not leave without receiving and giving hugs and saying "I love you." All phone calls are ended with "I love you." Yes, I do work at it continuously. I am very happy to say I have been now been married for over forty years and now have an endless supply of hugs!!

After reading these experiences, there may be things that you may have wished were different in your life. You can have it. Things can be overcome and changed. A lot you probably have had to learn on your own, even how to show different emotions in many ways.

So many foster children go through life wishing for more, and accepting just enough. Being complacent in the existence you have because of how you feel.

You have the choice and the power to make a difference in your life. A life coach can and will work with you. You tell your coach the topic and tell them what you would like to accomplish. Your life coach will work with you to come up with a plan on how to make your changes happen. Your coach will help you set up some accountability markers to ensure the success of your plan. Your coach will always be there for you along your journey. I can be that coach.

Tim Rahija

Tim Rahija is an aspiring entrepreneur, international author and business consultant, with prior professional experience in Law Enforcement, United States Army, Human Resource Management, Information Technology, and Aviation Maintenance. He is Founder/ CEO of his mobile application development company, Dreamscape Mobile Technology, started in 2012. He has been involved in additional business ventures in other technology platforms and life coaching and personal development, based on personal life altering experiences, challenges, studies and training. Tim earned a B.A. in Human Resource Management from Mid America Nazarene College in 1989, and graduated summa cum laude from DeVry University with a B.Sc. in Information Technology in 2004.

www.21st-century-mobile.com

www.appreneur2013.tumblr.com

✉ timothy.rahija@gmail.com

f facebook.com/timrahija

f facebook.com/pages/Live-a-Life-by-Design/259728190859117

f facebook.com/pages/Tim-Rahija-Capitalizing-on-Mobile-Technology/362746417078320

🐦 @MobileAppIncome

📌 pinterest.com/timrahija

in linkedin.com/pub/tim-rahija/48/704/70b

CHAPTER 8

IN THE BLINK OF AN EYE: THE WORLD I KNEW CHANGED

By Tim Rahija

In June 2010, I moved to Texas to begin a new career in aviation. I was on top of the world. I had finally reached a major career goal after working extremely hard for the previous two years and was now working for a top company in aviation. I was very happy and proud of what I had accomplished and was thrilled to be doing what I had once dreamed of. I thought life couldn't get any better.

On Sunday, September 5, 2010, I had been out on my motorcycle and had been out with some friends that evening, enjoying a holiday weekend. I remember parting company and stopping by the store on the way home with the plan of spending the rest of a fun evening enjoying some quiet time. I was on my way home when, in the blink of an eye, my life took a drastic, major unexpected turn. The next thing I remember was waking up in ICU in Temple, Texas, with a tube down my throat, vision in my right eye significantly impaired and partially taped shut, my right leg in a cast from the knee down, and numerous lacerations and stitches in my hands and arms.

Right before waking up, I remember being in what felt like a dream state, and a vagueness of feeling myself on the ground, and it was dark and someone was trying to talk to me, asking me questions and me trying to answer that person. The next part was hearing a noisy commotion around me and being in an ambulance and the feeling of struggling to breathe, and a bright light above me with an EMT leaning over me and in a forceful voice saying, "Stay with me Tim, stay with me," and the sound of the siren in the background. The next thing I remember was awakening to the sound of someone praying out loud for me and to see my dad and one of my co-workers at the foot of my bed. My initial reaction was nothing short of heart pounding panic. I was in excruciating pain, had a tube down my throat and couldn't speak, and I could barely see. I could tell I was in the hospital but had no clue of how I got there. Obviously, something very drastic and traumatic had happened. My Dad told me that I had been struck by a vehicle and a moment later was lying in the intersection with a shattered right orbit, broken nose, broken jaw and numerous other facial fractures, cuts, lacerations, six broken ribs, a punctured lung, and compound fractures in my right foot. I was transported to a local hospital for emergency surgery and stabilization and then flown to Temple because it has a level one trauma center.

Needless to say, it was a shock to the system to learn what had happened as I had no memory of being struck – and I still don't to this day. I had no idea of the true extent of my injuries, but I was alive and I thanked God for that simple fact. What was obviously crystal clear was that I was here by the grace of God for a reason, even though I had no idea why. I had no idea of what else there was to come. I knew that I was in more pain than I had ever experienced in my entire life. I was going to have at least two more surgeries; one for facial reconstruction and the other for my foot. I told myself that I had two choices; "You can ask 'Why me, why do I deserve this?' and be mired in self-pity, and wonder how this is going to affect your career and the rest of your life. OR simply accept what has happened and harness the power you know is within you and figure out a way to move forward, get healed, return to work and get on with your life."

I remember thinking the choice was simple and obvious. I had been through tough times and circumstances before, but I had NEVER given up. I CHOSE to accept the situation because of my faith in God and belief that things happen according to his plan and that if God brings us to it, he will bring us through it. I chose to take ownership of my circumstances and make them my own and do something positive, as giving up and quitting was NOT an option. Nor was I going to allow myself to feel a need to "get even" with or judge the individual that made a critical error in judgment and almost killed me. I was going to refuse to be consumed with negative energy and thus refuse to give away my power. Additionally, I didn't have pessimistic or negative thinking people to influence my thinking or decisions, which was a blessing.

It was here that I took a big negative and turned it into a huge positive by tapping into the vast, unlimited potential within. After getting out of the hospital, I got back in contact with a co-worker who had shared a business opportunity with me prior to the accident and got my own business going. I decided I was not going to let anything hold me back physically or psychologically.

Here are the primary points I want to share with and impress upon everyone. I had no control over the injuries I had sustained or the lack of mobility. But, what I DID have control over was how I chose to respond to those events. I will tell you from experience that you can do whatever YOU decide and choose upon. Nothing can keep you from achieving whatever you desire unless you allow it. I'm human just like anyone else, and if I was able to take a painful, negative, and traumatic experience and turn it into an enormous, positive experience that allowed me to make significant personal growth and learn so much more about myself and serve as an inspiration to others, then so can YOU. I had gone from being perhaps just a few heartbeats from death, unable to walk and in constant pain management, to walking without assistance by early December, then returning to work without restriction by mid-January 2011. I even bought a new motorcycle a few months later. That is the power of mindset, faith, and belief in a nutshell. What you focus on is what you create and determines your reality. My advice to all is to refuse to allow life's challenges stop you from achieving. Confront those challenges head-on and strongly envision yourself demolishing them. Your subconscious will make it happen.

I want to take these same principles and apply them to what we do in every aspect of life and what our "Why" is. We all encounter difficulties in life. Do NOT let those become an excuse to give up and quit, just because the road gets bumpy. Change your thoughts and you change your life. Maintain passion and laser beam focus and resolve. Remember that nothing of value comes easy or quick. Life is a marathon, not a sprint. The key is to get clear life vision and purpose, develop a plan and strategy, establish a pace and work that plan. The ONLY person, who has the power to defeat you is YOU.

Here are some other things that I have learned and want to share. Ask yourself what is stopping you from getting what you want? Who YOU are always determines what YOU get. Is there something that you do or don't do consistently on a daily basis that has been stopping you from having and living the life that you know deep down you deserve and God wants for you? God did NOT create you for a life of mediocrity. What habit or habits stand in your way? Could it be things like fear, procrastination, complacency, pride or ego? What mindsets and beliefs do you have that are adopted from parents, peers, friends or others as a result of conditioning or programming that don't serve you? What color are the lenses through which you see the world? What beliefs do you possess that are holding you back?

Take a serious, but honest personal inventory of these things within and make a plan for change. If you can't figure any of this out and come up with answers, then you may be in denial. Truly effective, successful people can identify what they need to change to make themselves more effective. This process is called self-awareness. When you truly become self-aware, the obvious changes needed are revealed to you. Don't limit your challenges; challenge your limits. And, if at any time you feel you need special help along the way, do what I did and simply ask God. He is the constant support, especially in difficult times.

Jill Gjorgjievski

Jill Gjorgjievski is a Multi-Dimensional Healer/Teacher | RN | Early Childhood Teacher | Certified Intuitive Life Coach | International Author. She is a Master in Angelic Reiki, Unicorn Healing Energy, Faery Reiki, with the power of Love Energy Healing and she teaches these modalities.

Jill Gjorgjievski is the founding CEO / Director of Gjorgjievski Enterprises, with the power of Love, Chocolates and Things. Her vision and mission in life is to help people achieve balance and success in life using the highest vibration of love.

www.jgjorgjievski.com

www.jillgjorgjievski.com

www.withthepoweroflove.com

Ⓢ Jill.Gjorgjievski

✉ jgjorgjievski@yahoo.com.au

❶ facebook/jillgjorgjievski

g+ plus.google.com/102253108963879351612/about

in linkedin.com/au.linkedin.com/pub/jill-gjorgjievski80|82b|929

CHAPTER 9

LIFTING MY SPIRIT OUT OF THE DEPTHS OF DESPAIR

By Jill Gjorgjievski

If you're like many women, chances are you go to great lengths not to burden those around you. I was no different, but the signs of stroke demand immediate attention, even if it seems like the worst possible timing.

I remember the night I experienced symptoms of my stroke like it was yesterday. I was sitting at my kitchen table looking out into the darkness, recalling the events of the day. I had just buried my husband and soulmate. I started getting hot, began sweating. I had chest tightness as if my heart was in a vise.

I had never felt so scared and anxious at the same time in my life. I was acting like I was completely ignorant of what was taking place. When my vision began to blur and I was unable to hold my cup of coffee, I told myself that it was normal to close up and not to feel anything.

My brain started to scream at me, I saw inside my head the sign "alarm" in neon lights "you are having a stroke." I said to my conscience, "No! I'm not! I'm just feeling numb – what do you expect? I just buried my best friend – the only person in the world I could talk to and trust." Feeling sorry for myself I continued to stare out the window my body stiff and rigid, trying to keep some control of myself. Then I heard a soft voice outside of my head that whispered in my right ear, "You are having a stroke Jill, but it will be alright if you allow us to help you." At that point my nursing instincts took control and I realized I had nothing in the house that would help if I was actually having a stroke. My brain still screaming for me to take

64

something for the stroke, I mentally answered the voice, "Ok so help me." The voice told me to relax and allow myself to slide to the floor. I did this, but before I allowed myself to slide down to the floor I took some over the counter medication to help relax me. The rest I don't remember.

I was awakened like from a sleep by the soft voice telling me to slowly get up and sit back in the chair. At first I didn't realize what had just happened. I felt fine on the floor like I had a good night's sleep but as I went to get up my head throbbed like I had been drinking, my legs felt weak, and I could not stand up. It was a struggle, as my arms felt weak as well. Feeling like I had a hangover I thought to myself, "Well that medication had a good punch to it," while smiling to myself; but in fact I was weak because of the stroke. I went to pick up my cup only to have it slide through my hands; I had no feeling from the wrist down. At this point I started to panic a little, self-sabotaging thoughts like, "You're for the scrap heap now, no one is going to want you, and all the hard work was for nothing," crept in. I realized that I had lost the will to live and didn't care what happened to me. Although the spirit within me was screaming at me, giving me instructions on how to overcome this, I refused to listen.

In the days that followed, I did my best to hide my symptoms from my children, but they noticed that I couldn't hold anything or eat anything, which made them question me. They tried to convince me to go to the doctor, but I did not listen. I was too busy being stubborn and thinking what would happen if I was properly diagnosed as having a stroke. They had, without my knowledge, gone to the family doctor on my behalf but I would not budge. My eldest daughter then tried speaking to close family friends to come and speak to me in order for me to seek help.

Crunch time came or – if you like – a wakeup call, when one day my daughter came home all excited that she had bought me hair color and exclaimed that it was pamper night and she was going to pamper me and color my hair. I got angry and stated to her that coloring my hair was superficial and pointless since I felt worthless. She was determined; she responded back at me, "Please mum, I don't want you to be like the old widowed ladies. I want my classy mum back."

Her words penetrated the wall of stubbornness I had put up for protection, and for days afterwards her words played in my head. I realized that I needed to dig deep and find my inner strength again, if not for myself, for my children. This spurred me on to dig deep into my feelings and find the fighting spirit within me again.

Together with my children's support and my guardian angels by my side guiding me, I started on the path that led me back to health. For the next three months, this became a daily routine of healing. With each healing session, I had to dig deep and have faith that I would be able to find my inner spirit again to, fight the physical and emotional limitations I was experiencing, trusting that all would be well. At times this was not easy for me to do; I became overwhelmed to the point of being stifled and stuck as I peeled the layers of emotions that are associated with the loss of a loved one and surviving a stroke. With determination and a fighting spirit I slowly regained feelings in my hands, my vision became clearer, my swallowing improved, and I was no longer choking on anything. My facial droop took longer to heal, but there was improvement and within three months I was well enough to get back to my normal routine with the business.

Dig Yourself out of your own Despair:

Whatever life gives you, even if it hurts, be strong and act like the way you always do. Because strong walls shake but never collapse. Obstacles don't have to stop you! If you run into a wall, don't turn around and give up. Figure out how to climb it, go through it or work around it. Find that one thing that will reignite your inner spark -that one thing that is your driving force – and focus on it as you go through your challenge.

In our physical experience, it is important to take the time to develop our emotions. The thoughts we use to create our reality are shaded by emotional participation of our consciousness. Always attempt to align your emotional responses with actions rather than reaction. This way the participation is fully created from your core rather than another's.

Recognize the power emotions emanate whether they are positive or negative. Letting them run rampant is not a good use of the energy.

Learning to balance them within will lead to a better created reality. Always remember that the beauty you have will radiate and shine through you in many ways, to touch the hearts and souls of many. You are the beautiful creature that is surviving in this world of madness; knowing that you can survive and hold a smile on your face, and love in your heart is one thing that you are to be grateful for. However there are many things to be grateful for. It's about honoring the self within you, the courage within your being and finding the strength to face each day when times are tough.

You are a gift to yourself and you are the present that needs to be opened daily. But with that it is allowing the heart to be opened to that you may fear, by those who may hurt you and step into that space of vulnerability. For you are the savior to your own graces, you are the bandage to your own wound, you are the beat to your own heart and you are the song to your own dance.

An emotional component exists in all of us. It is for you to decide how much to let it show. Know, however, that it does exist in every one of us. Engage it, Act within it. Become a more colorful creator; a full spectrum is available, however you should decide to use it. It can be volatile, but in that energy, quite remarkable.

Take that step into beyond and know that you have the support and love of the Divine Spirit and know that you will always be blessed. Just allow and be the brightness that you choose to be in this world.

Signs of a stroke demand immediate attention, even if it seems like the worst possible timing or possible environmental side effects. Seek medical attention immediately; call your local emergency service at the first signs of stroke.

The information offered in this chapter is intended to be general information based on my own experience and general life issues. Information is offered in good faith; however you are under no obligation to use this information. It is not meant to replace professional medical advice.

Sarah Dickinson Bailey

Sarah Bailey is an international author, entrepreneur, and business consultant. She first worked as a registered dietician in major teaching hospitals, nursing homes, and in corporate nutrition. After staying home full-time with kids for 9 years, she became passionate about growing a home business, teaching others how to create the incomes and life they desire, right from the comfort of their own homes. She believes in living life to the fullest now, (not waiting until retirement) and showing others how they can do the same. She lives in Connecticut with her loving husband and two very fun growing boys.

SarahDBailey.com

 facebook.com/SarahDickinsonBailey

 twitter.com/SarahBaileyB

CHAPTER 10

HOW A POSITIVE MINDSET HELPED ME HEAL FROM NECK CANCER

By Sarah Dickinson Bailey

"Focus on the health you want, not the illness you don't!"

~Sarah D. Bailey

On December 3, 2012, when my surgeon uttered the words "We found cancer," a few things went through my mind. I was still a little groggy from the anesthesia. After all, I was still in the recovery room from what was supposed to be a simple surgery to remove a harmless cyst in my neck, but the doctors at Yale Medical Center found tumor cells in one of my lymph nodes. Before surgery, I had MRI and CT scans and biopsies, and they were all negative, so needless to say, I was at the same time shocked, confused and upset upon hearing this news.

I know the news of cancer is devastating to many people. Had I found out about it weeks before surgery, I might have been a little more freaked out about it, but I didn't have time for that. I barely had enough time to process the information before we were planning the next phase of treatment, which was to do six weeks of daily radiation treatments. I refused to do chemotherapy, because I just didn't want to have those toxins in my body, but also, with the type of cancer I had, going through chemo wouldn't have improved my outcome much at all.

I never asked myself, "Why me?" because, I learned many years ago to ask instead, "Why not me?" I mean, what makes me so special that nothing bad should ever happen to me? An even better question is, "What can I learn from this experience?" or "How can I be refined during this process?"

Since I know a little bit about the power of the mind, I decided almost immediately that I wasn't going to let cancer become my identity. I took the attitude that I was going to conquer cancer. I realized that the treatments and the side effects were going to be painful, but it was just something I had to get through. There's way too much for me still to do on this earth to be held back by cancer. My "I Will Conquer" attitude, my faith, and supportive family and friends got me through the whole process.

It was only six weeks after surgery that we started six weeks of daily radiation to my head and neck. My fear of the cancer paled in comparison to the fears I had of having my head strapped down to a metal table with a plastic mesh mask tightly molded to my face, while they shot radiation through me, knowing that with each treatment, my side effects would worsen daily. After only 2 weeks of radiation, the blisters on my tongue, mouth and throat, and difficulty swallowing even my own saliva, resulted in a feeding tube being placed in my stomach.

The side effects were painful, but my spirits were high, because I knew it was a trial I had to endure. Sometimes I just had to focus on getting through that day.

There were lessons for me to learn that I wouldn't be able to learn any other way. I decided to look for those lessons and have gratitude for the many, many blessings in my life. Every day when I had my head strapped down to the table, and I started to feel claustrophobic, I would think of all the things I was grateful for, such as: family, friends, radiation staff, technology to treat this cancer, heat in the building, a sterile environment, a tile floor (instead of a dirt floor in another country), electricity for lighting, and so on.

Here is something I know about the Law of Attraction: we get what we focus on most of the time. Whatever we think about, we draw to us. This Law of Attraction is as true as the Law of Gravity. Knowing this, I was able to keep my thoughts on what I wanted, not what I didn't want. The Bible tells us, "As a man thinketh, so also he is." So we are what we think we are.

Sympathy from others was something I didn't want. I desired their encouragement and thoughts of healing instead. Because if they said, "I'm sorry you are going through all this, and you must feel miserable," I would have focused on the pain and the illness. I wanted people to give me words of healing, because that's where I wanted my focus to be.

The only thing I wanted to draw to me was good health. Every day I focused on the good and exceptional health that I wanted, not the illness that I didn't want. Sometimes it was tough to do this when I was feeling crummy, but I did it anyway. I am now one year out from surgery and treatments, and so far, the doctors tell me there is no evidence of cancer and it's very unlikely it will return. I attribute much of that to a strong mindset.

One lesson I learned is to be more present in each situation I'm in, and to not be distracted. When I'm with family, I focus on my family, make eye contact with them when speaking to them, not texting my business partners or friends or worrying about all the other things I could be doing. And when I'm working my home business, helping others to achieve their goals, I focus on that and try not to get distracted. A divided mind does not serve anyone.

Another lesson I learned is that life is too short for us to be limited by our fears and to be afraid to take some risks. Too many people reach the end of their lives with regrets for the things they did not do. My passion is to live life to the fullest, to take chances, overcome my fears, and live up to the potential that God gave me, so that when I get to the end of my life, I can look back and say, "Yeah, that was a life well-lived." Another passion of mine is to work with others, to help them achieve the same results.

All in all, I am grateful for my cancer journey. It was completely miserable at times, but I always knew I'd learn something from it. That God would redirect my path somehow, and draw me closer to Him and my family. It cultivated me to be the wife, mom and business leader that God created me to be. I wouldn't have experienced this level of growth without this experience.

Whatever your trial is, whether it's a health, relationship, or work situation, I challenge you to take a step back and ask yourself a few questions:

- Instead of "Why me?" ask yourself, "Why not me?"
- "What lessons am I supposed to learn as a result of going through this trial?"
- "How am I being refined?"
- "How might I be able to serve others as a result of this experience?"

Sometimes God can only get our attention by strapping us down with an illness or life obstacle. Oftentimes, it takes a painful experience that causes us to step back and evaluate what we are doing, and where we are going.

Your focus should not be on the obstacles holding you back. Instead, allow the obstacle to teach you and refine you into the person, the leader, the mom or the dad, the friend, the brother, the sister, the daughter or son that you were called to be. Each one of us was given different gifts and talents, and it is up to us to figure out what they are and to use them to the best of our abilities. Find out what it is you are called to do.

As you go through your trials, be very aware of your mindset. Refuse to let an illness or an obstacle become your identity. The Law of Attraction, says that like attracts like. If you put out negative thoughts, like "Why am I always sick?" then you will continue to have illness. Instead, focus on the end result you desire (strong health, strong marriage, success in business, living your dream life), so you can draw that to you.

Realize that you have way too many things to do on this earth than to be burdened with this trial. Know that you will be a stronger person on the other side of it. Going through these experiences will position you to mentor and help people who go through a similar experience.

Move forward in the direction of your dreams. Obstacles will certainly meet you in your path. But YOU get to decide what you do with them. Let the obstacles refine you into the person you are called to be. Don't let them cause you to give up. Don't give up....step UP!!

Anita Sechesky

Anita is a Registered Nurse, Certified Life Coach, International Best Selling Author, Speaker, Trainer, NLP and LOA Wealth Practitioner, as well as Big Vision Consultant. She studied Marketing at the School of Online Business and completed her Advanced Certificate of Life Coaching at Academy of Coaching Cognition. She is the CEO and Owner of Anita Sechesky – Living Without Limitations. Anita has assisted many people breaking through their own limiting beliefs in life and business. She has two International Best Sellers and is compiling her third anthology "Living Without Limitations – 30 Stories to Love Your World," to be released in 2014.

You can contact Anita at the following:

www.anitasechesky.com

🅢 anita.sechesky

✉ asechesky@hotmail.ca

🅕 facebook.com/AnitaSechesky

🅕 facebook.com/asechesky

🅞 @nursie4u

🅟 pinterest.com/anitasechesky

🅛 ca.linkedin.com/pub/anita-sechesky/3b/111/8b9

CHAPTER 11

THE HUMAN MIND

By Anita Sechesky

Our mind is the control center for the entire body, and it initiates the actions and reactions of life around us. Many people have yet to come to the knowledge and awareness of how powerful our minds really can be. Every thought we create has the profound ability to affect our lives, as these ideas become a blueprint for our minds to focus on and move forward in that direction.

Our physical responses react to our thoughts. We can literally make ourselves happy or sad and follow through with those behaviors. Since we do not know the future, why do we often think about the worst possible outcome? It is more beneficial to focus on and create positive thoughts that encourage our bodies not to have any stress or tension.

Throughout my nursing career, I have witnessed so many individuals worrying about future events they had absolutely no control over. Anxiety only causes tension, increased heart rate, frustration and plain old stress! Many physicians would agree that it can even lead to complicated health issues if left unattended. Every area of our lives can be affected, from poor eating habits to bad decision making, relationship issues, insomnia, and even productivity in the workplace. Who wants that?

We all have the ability to change the direction of our lives. We really can create our reality by the negative and positive thoughts that we think about. I know you can imagine all the ways that your life could be better right now. So go ahead and keep thinking better thoughts! Keep dreaming and keep focusing! Let go of all the false beliefs you thought were wasting your time in the past and start planning for the life you really want, by using your mind to discover the best ways to make it happen. Are you where you want to be in life right now? If you are, then good for you! If you aren't and believe you may be stuck in a rut, you can still change your destiny. Yes! You can change it and you can continue to adjust the way that you want to respond to life.

What you focus on becomes your reality! What are you thinking about at this very moment? If your thoughts are about worry, then you will always have something more to be anxious about. But if your thoughts are on problem solving, then you have a positive outlook and you will always find the answer that will work for you. Where there is a will there is always a way. Many times in life we do not even realize we are our own worst enemy. The reason I say this is because if we continue to allow others to harm, betray or disrespect our dignity, we are letting ourselves down; no one else! You see, we subconsciously choose the life we have. We all have choices to make and we determine the outcome of our decisions by what we really want or choose to avoid. When we have a sound and knowledgeable mind to make right or wrong decisions to fit our present circumstances, we become responsible for how things are in our lives. Sometimes it may be as simple as just needing to fall in love with ourselves all over again. Many may not even understand what I am saying, but it is a very healthy thing to discover that you love yourself and the life that you have.

Once you begin to accept the circumstances in your world, you will see the details with a renewed perspective. It may be that the life you once thought was so horrible is not so bad after all. For some, it might be a wakeup call to discover their best life yet! Either way, loving oneself can sometimes be compared to Godliness, as God created you in HIS image. Be thankful you were created as the beautiful, handsome, and wonderful human being that you are. After all, you could have ended up being on the other end of the food chain!

As a nurse, I have met so many people and I have seen how people in general have so much on their minds. They are filled with so many responsibilities and duties that they do not even know how to enjoy life. They end up coming into the hospital with some kind of ailment or infirmity. Their daily tasks have become overwhelming and they just lose that spark of life. You see, they have allowed life and all of its negative crap to just pile up and become such a burden that it is next to impossible to find the sunshine on a cloudy day. They may even have developed a stress related illness, another thing to worry about on top of everything else.

We all have roles and responsibilities, but is it fair to make yourself forget how fun and carefree life can be? Many times it can be just as simple as taking the time to relax once in a while. Yes, there will always be things to do, but I often wonder why people get so bent out of shape because they have to take the garbage out or maybe do something extra today. What about the grumpy co-worker who just doesn't care about who they offend or hurt?

Our minds have the ability to block out all of these negative events and its effects in life if we want to or choose to. Trust me, I have been there and I have had to do this exact same thing. Yes, I made up my mind that I would be positive and not attract anything harmful into my world. Besides, I did not want that draining, negative energy to come near me and make my day stressful. As a nurse, I had to learn how to keep from soaking it up. By doing so, I remained calm and full of peace, positivity, and smiles! In healthcare, there are many opportunities to do this very thing when working with so many people who carry their emotional baggage into every room they walk into. I encourage you to stop being an emotional sponge; your mind has the ability to create more of what you want in your life. What you focus on can become your reality!

Here are some more tips to help heal your mind and keep it healthy:

- Let go of all the things from your past that do not empower you to become a better person.
- Let go of relationships that are verbally damaging.
- Let go of addictions that may be keeping you in a state of dependence.
- Let go of negative self-talk.
- Let go of the reasons why you think you don't deserve better.
- Let go of self-hate and self-abuse.

- Let go of painful memories.
- Let go of what does not serve you any longer.
- Let go of lost hope.
- Let go of social activities that attract nonsense.
- Let go of abusive relationships.
- Let go of the words that others have spoken against you.
- Let go of the painful memories you keep replaying in your mind.
- Let go of all the lies told by others.
- Let go of fears.
- Let go of rejection.
- Let go of places that remind you of painful events.
- Let go of pictures and memories from past broken relationships.
- Let go of things that remind you of failures.
- Let go of the past; it is not where you are going.

Here are some things you will want to remember to keep your mind healthy:

- Receive love!
- Give love!
- Forgive yourself.
- Forgive others.
- Show appreciation to others.
- Think Success!
- Associate with Positivity!
- Discover new and healthy relationships!
- Be kind to yourself.
- Be your Best Friend Forever!
- Read inspirational material.
- Attend things you enjoy.

- Pursue your passions.
- Give yourself a chance to make mistakes; you are only human.
- Learn to laugh at yourself, and then laugh every day.
- Live light-heartedly.
- Listen to uplifting music.
- Read the comics.
- Observe the elderly.
- Watch your children and learn how to enjoy life through the eyes of a child.
- Spend more time with your family.
- Spend more time with your parents.
- Assess your relationships and discover the draining ones.
- Make the right decisions that you have been putting off for so long.
- Be confident!
- Understand yourself.
- Research your doubts.
- Share your life with those you care about.

I urge you to take control of your mind. Don't just let life happen to you. Steer it in the direction that you want it to go. Refocus and zoom in on your long lost goals. Examine the lives of others that you admire and observe their behaviors and choices closely. Let life show you how you can succeed and make things happen effortlessly without the stress and turmoil of ignorance.

You are a highly intelligent creature with a powerful mind. You are capable of moving forward successfully. Failures can become a stepping stone to learn from your past mistakes. Be mindful. Allow yourself the room to grow into your best self yet!

Kaila Janes

Kaila Janes is a certified Law of Attraction Practitioner, International Author, Inspirational Speaker and Motivational Trainer. Kaila enjoys working with young people to inspire and motivate and encourage them about the power and healing of self-love and acceptance. Currently she is writing a novel about her life and the hurdles that she has had to overcome. Kaila Janes enjoys writing and finding ways to make a difference in people's lives. Her other interests include singing and anything music related. Kaila loves to laugh and truly believes laughter is the best medicine.

You can connect with Kaila Janes at:

www.kailajanes.wordpress.com

✉ contactkailajanes@gmail.com

ⓕ facebook.com/kailajanes

ⓧ twitter.com/godsmonkey22

▶ youtube.com/godsmonkey23

CHAPTER 12

I AM A SOUL SURVIVOR: HEALING FROM DEPRESSION AND SELF-ABUSE

By Kaila Janes

Depression is often a life filled with silence. Some may think that depression is deliberately chosen. It is just a way you think or feel. That it can be changed just by thinking or feeling different. This is not the truth. I have lived with depression for 11 years. I know what it is like to be taken over by the feelings it brings upon the person who suffers from it. I have lived through the days where all I wanted to do was lie in bed and shut the world out. I know what it's like to hit rock bottom.

As a Christian, I would wear masks which hide the sadness. It was all because I feared being judged. Aren't Christians supposed to be happy people? Don't they have God on their side? While this may be true, God doesn't cause depression. It is an imbalance within and can affect anyone of any age, religion or race just the same. It doesn't pick and choose one person over another.

Most of my life I just wanted to crawl into a hole, curl up and disappear. Spending my life faking happiness and smiling when deep down all I felt was despair was the most difficult show to put on. One of my loved ones once said to me, "You have failed in life!" This statement stabbed me in the heart to the deepest core, making me only shut down further. The emotional pain of those words was so intense, I didn't truly know how to deal with them or cope with the effects they created within.

The depression began to take over my entire life and I began finding release in cutting. At first it started slowly. Then there were days I would get so depressed that all I could think about was cutting my wrist. There was one night in particular that stands out in my mind. Family drama swirled around, engulfing me in negativity. I felt so defeated, all alone; like no one cared I was even there. I sat on my bedroom floor, darkness surrounding me, knife in my hands. I just cried out to God to take my life! I didn't want to be a part of this world any longer.

It was a nonstop battle in my mind. The smallest things would seem to trigger it. Whether it be my parents fighting, someone yelling at me, loved ones moving away, or even having a broken family, it created the perfect storm within. Being an emotional sensitive type of person, I didn't have the tools to adequately deal with these situations in a healthy manner. I would tend to bottle everything up inside instead of reaching out for help from others. Even when I did, it seemed to get me nowhere. Unfortunately, the only way I found relief was cutting.

At age 24 I started my first medication. After three days I stopped. I didn't like the side effects, how the medication made me feel. It drained me of every ounce of energy, which only kept me in the depressed state. There were days I felt like a hypocrite. Here I was supposed to be living a Godly life and yet many nights I found myself trying to think of ways to end the precious life He had given to me. Scars were created by my actions. These scars were the most difficult evidence of my depression to hide. Even though I never made really deep cuts, they were still quite noticeable.

Men were a source of great pain for me, starting with my father. The pain carried through into my relationships and friendships with other men as I grew up. I found myself giving my heart away to people who claimed they were friends but really in the end only wanted one thing. It caused my heart deep pain to know that someone I loved so deeply didn't love me back. It made me feel unwanted, unacceptable and lonely. I tried to fill the void within me with relationships, but the heartache was only another source that dragged me further into my depressive state.

My life was going in a downward spiral, and I felt all I could do was watch it happen. My faith started to crumble, I felt so far from God. I didn't know who I was anymore. My life was a battlefield! I didn't know which battles to continue to fight and which ones to just give into.

Depression isn't the end of my story. It doesn't define who I am and it doesn't define who you are either. It is a condition, but it is not who you are! Living with depression and self-injury has made me a stronger person. It gave me a drive to help others. I look at my life just a year ago and I can't even imagine that I would be in the place I am now. The transformational journey is where I live currently. It is a path. The temptation to cut is there, just like any addiction or condition, but I have learned coping mechanisms. I have a support system I am always building around me. They lift me up and listen intently to what I have to say no matter what. I am not judged, just accepted, which gives me the endurance to push through to fight back. There are so many people in my life who love me and see something special when they look at me. I learned to stop being so hard on myself. I learned that I have a great personality, am worthy of so much more than I know, and am a person full of laughter. I deserve happiness; I deserve to shine, just as you who read this do! Sometimes we may be our own worst enemies.

I have been given the opportunity to reach out to others by sharing my story. Survival would not have happened if I hadn't noticed the need for love. Not the love of a man but the love of my heavenly father. Words carry more power than you know. Words can help save a life; they can build people up or tear them down. It took me a long time to realize just how important it was to forgive myself and to ask for the Lord's forgiveness. I needed to love myself in order to truly love those around me. Change doesn't happen overnight. It takes small steps. Even if you have to wake up every morning, look in the mirror and say, "I am worth it," or "Thank you Lord for life today," it makes a difference. Every small action leads to larger actions.

Many roadblocks have been placed before me along my healing journey. I know there is light at the end of the tunnel; I can see it shinning in my life. There is hope! Believe it! No matter how difficult it may seem right now, this is only but a moment, and change takes just that one step in the direction you want to go. Surround yourself with people who encourage you and lift you up. Positivity breeds positivity and negativity breeds negativity. Think of your dreams and the things you want in life. Make those dreams a reality! It is possible!

I will not let depression or cutting control my life. I am worth the fight. The scars I bear only remind me that the Lord is the reason I am alive today. I am a survivor and that will never change.

5 steps you can take immediately to begin a life of change!

1. Isolation is desolation! Do not stay isolated! Surround yourself with positive people, people who listen and love you no matter what.

2. Professionals are there to help you. Seek out a counselor, psychologist or life coach for your specific needs. A family doctor can help point you in the right direction, if you don't know where to start.

3. Find healthy ways in which to express yourself. Ways that can bring you happiness within and fill that void. Examples can be music, writing, movies, etc.

4. If you feel the need to cut or do other self-destructive behaviors, reach out to your support network. Don't be alone or isolate yourself.

5. Get involved in your community through youth groups, or other church groups. Being involved in your community can create a sense of accomplishment.

Remember to live, love and laugh! You are not alone in this fight. There are others who struggle just like you. It is time to break those chains that bind you and live a life of freedom! The life God truly created for you. There is a plan for you, your life is worth living and change is one step towards a different destination. Be the change, be the voice, don't let your life be defined by where you have been.

Anita Sechesky

Anita is a Registered Nurse, Certified Life Coach, International Best Selling Author, Speaker, Trainer, NLP and LOA Wealth Practitioner, as well as Big Vision Consultant. She studied Marketing at the School of Online Business and completed her Advanced Certificate of Life Coaching at Academy of Coaching Cognition. She is the CEO and Owner of Anita Sechesky – Living Without Limitations. Anita has assisted many people breaking through their own limiting beliefs in life and business. She has two International Best Sellers and is compiling her third anthology "Living Without Limitations – 30 Stories to Love Your World," to be released in 2014.

You can contact Anita at the following:

www.anitasechesky.com

🅢 anita.sechesky

✉ asechesky@hotmail.ca

🅕 facebook.com/AnitaSechesky

🅕 facebook.com/asechesky

🅞 @nursie4u

🅟 pinterest.com/anitasechesky

🅛 ca.linkedin.com/pub/anita-sechesky/3b/111/8b9

CHAPTER 13

YES, I CAN BE SWEET AS CHOCOLATE
By Anita Sechesky

When I was growing up in Terrace Bay, a small community in Northwestern Ontario, I recall wondering, "Why did we come here?" I will never forget the early years of feeling like I didn't belong or fit in, growing up in such an isolated part of Canada.

I was born in Georgetown, in the exotic and tropical country of British Guyana. My family relocated to the extreme cold winter climate of Canada when I was only four years old. This was my first major life transition. I can still remember being in the change room in public school with all the girls looming over me because I had pierced ears. I guess at that time it wasn't a Canadian "thing" for little girls to have their ears pierced at such an early age. They kept asking me what kind of language I was speaking since my Guyanese accent was very different to them. Even though they understood me, they questioned everything I was saying. Some of my classmates would even stand next to me and compare their pale skin to my golden brown skin tone. "Yes, I was the new kid in town and I was Brown." I recall being placed one year ahead of my Canadian peers in class because when I lived in Georgetown, I had already attended nursery school so I knew my "ABCs," "123s" and cursive writing. I was left-handed by birth, but had to change and learn to write with my right hand because this is what was expected.

The novelty of being the new kid eventually wore off, and they just ignored me. No child should ever feel isolated or alone. I recall many times walking home by myself and talking to Jesus. HE was my best friend and never let me down. I remember during recesses being the only one out on the school grounds by myself. All the other kids kept to themselves, playing at the other end of the school yard. I was never invited to join them. That was when the "Lonely Years" began for me in Grades 4 and 5. Ironically, it was a period in my life that I made a significant discovery of my life's purpose. From this age, I decided that when I grew up, I wanted to be a Registered Nurse just like my late aunt. Despite being teased by a few of my classmates because of the color of my skin, or being called "Brownie" or "Chocolate," I felt sorry for these people. They didn't understand that despite our exterior differences, all people from all over the world had the same emotions and feelings, and therefore deserved to be treated equally. What a profound discovery at such a young age. I strongly believe that I owe my philosophical views on life to my mom and dad, who themselves were dealing with adult ignorance in a small "white" community. Many people in this part of the country had no shame in their outward prejudices or indifference to something that was not like them. My parents taught me to forgive others despite the circumstances we faced.

When I was nine years old, my cousins from Toronto moved in with us. I remember asking my older cousin, as she was making these amazing chocolate cookies with REAL chocolate bars, "Why do they call me Chocolate?" She smiled at me and said, "Because you are so sweet Anita!" and gave me a hug. That is a moment I will never forget. Yes I am sweet and yes I can be smart.

If you ask me what was the worst, I would have to say that my bad days were the lonely times I spent by myself. When the other kids were invited to birthday parties, my invitation never seemed to arrive. One specific time, I remember my neighbor across the street from where I grew up looked like he invited the entire class at his house, except for me. It was a horrible feeling witnessing this, because I felt like I didn't fit in once again even though we were good friends when we were much younger. The only reason I mention this is because the previous years when his family first moved to town, we were great friends doing cartwheels on the front yard or just hanging out on our bikes with the other kids in the neighborhood. His family moved away and later that year, he came back for a visit. It was the last time I saw him, because a few weeks after he went home he died. This event left me realizing how fragile life really is, and that even though friendships may not last forever, the impact that we have on one another's lives last for eternity. My late childhood friend had shown me how easily our perceptions are influenced by others and despite everything, I could still be accepted for who I was regardless of where I came from.

When I got into the older grades, I am thankful for some very close and dear friends who helped me develop my unique personality. We had some great times together going through high school. As crazy as those days may have been as a teenager, joking and laughing, life felt more carefree, because I was learning how having a certain attitude of positivity can go a long way.

As the years went by, I realized that not all people were as nice and sweet as I thought. It is a sad testament to what many were exposed to and the ignorance they chose to stay in. My faith in God helped me through so many times when I did not understand even those who betrayed my loyalty in the Church. Many people may attend a church, but they may not always have the love of God within their hearts. Because of faith, I learned from an early age to forgive others – not because I was supposed to but because it really did make me feel better inside. It didn't matter if they were family, friends, people I knew, or complete strangers, I learned that no one has the right to make me feel badly for who I was because greater is He that is within my heart than what happens around me. This set the course and direction for my life. Without actively practicing the Love of God and applying forgiveness when needed, I could never have made it through some of the most hurtful experiences in my life.

For those of you who have experienced similar feelings of isolation, rejection, or racism, I want to encourage you. If you see a need for racial tolerance, approach your employer or community organizations and help new citizens integrate successfully. After all, each person brings a promise of hope and richness to society.

Just because you may not necessarily fit into the environment you are in right now, it doesn't mean that you can't flourish or become all that you were created to be. You are an incredible creation. There's only one of you: individual, unique, and wonderfully made. You have your own fingerprints, feelings, emotions, and memories. I urge you to let go of what harm others have said or acted out towards you. Ignorance is a weapon that many do not understand that causes division and turmoil.

Do not let the hatred of others take your joy away. Let go of things that do not allow you the freedom to love yourself. Seek out counsel when necessary and believe that not all people are the same. Many negative behaviors and attitudes are developed because of geographical locations and upbringing. Unfortunately, because not all individuals are educated enough to understand humanity, appreciation for different cultures is lacking within these people.

It's time to explore your heart. What is it that you desire in life? You've been given a chance to live the best life as you see fit. We all start from somewhere, but end up in a different place. Don't be so hard on yourself; you have greatness waiting to be discovered within. Listen to your heart, mind, body, and spirit. Let them be your compass for your greatest discovery. Reexamine your life. Where are you? Is it where you want to be? If it is, then why are you still unhappy? You can always start new tomorrow. Develop a game plan for your life. Set yourself up for success. Think baby steps, then you can leap tall buildings. Your healing begins now. Your past does not determine your future, in fact your past discovers your future if you use the pieces of your life as the stepping stones to your personal success. No matter what culture you are, you are the culture of God, our Creator, as you were created in HIS image. Love yourself. What better way to be your own BFF (Best Friend Forever). Now is the time to start dreaming, start believing, start praying, and start expecting great things to happen. It's about time; you deserve it.

I would love to work with you if you need a friend. As a Professional Life Coach, I can help you to move more quickly into the life of your dreams than if you were to walk this road alone.

Brian Baulch

Brian Baulch lives in Ballarat City, Victoria, Australia. Married for longer than eight years, without children yet. He is a certified Life Coach, Newspaper Printers Assistant, and Owner and Co-founder with his wife of Rechargelife and Fusiontourism. His expertise led him to coach and consult small travel tourism business owners and keen travelers in connecting their mission of life experience, expertise, passions, talents and skills and using information technology tools to share their unique life story. Brian thrives in reaching out to dreamers and clients seeking a meaningful and creative purpose life.

www.brianbaulch.com

www.enthuse.me/brianbaulch

🅢 brindel

✉ brianbaulch@gmail.com

🅕 facebook.com/brianbaulchcoach

🅕 facebook.com/BrianAndrewBaulch

🅣 twitter.com/BrianBaulch

🅟 pinterest.com/brianbaulch

🅖⁺ plus.google.com/+BrianBaulch

🅛 au.linkedin.com/in/brianbaulch

CHAPTER 14

I WAS ONLY SIXTEEN BUT I SURVIVED!

By Brian Baulch

In March 1988, the Autumn season for Australia, I was a spirited but shy sixteen year old boy who was eager to pursue all of what the school curriculum offered the students, however I was still undecided which career path to go for. I appreciated what they taught us in school such as outdoor recreational education, home economics, basic computer skills, electrical and electronics classes. The real dilemma was I had no driven passion for something desirable, which offered the old school system that geared me towards a career path.

I found my co-op job experience that I completed in the local hospital as a Hygienic Health Assistant (Cleaner) more enjoyable. I thought this was more fun than schooling. My career adviser requested an appointment after getting the report back from my job at how well the employer thought I performed. Unfortunately, the career adviser said they had no vacant job available in the cooking area at the hospital, which I wanted to try, as I did love to cook at home for the family.

Unexpectedly exciting news came from my career adviser that a local large bakery in my home city required an apprentice baker. For a minute, I did not know what to say. I had quick flash clashing through my mind to choose job or school. Finally, I agreed for an interview at the bakery, and they informed me about my job expectations. What stood out was they required someone to work nightshift. At the age of 16 years old, this was not the job I wanted to purse.

A few days passed, I had not heard from the employer about the apprenticeship or the result of my interview. I knew there were a few others going for this opportunity. Abruptly out of nowhere, I got a phone call asking if I would be ready to start on a certain date and time. Utterly gobsmacked for about 15 seconds, I agreed to willingly venture this apprenticeship probationary period of three months.

Unknowing at the time, I clinched the deal to my first future employer that would eventually lead to a fork in the road that would change my life, despite my uncertainty about career choice. This choice would reroute my life emotionally, mentally and spiritually.

It was prevalent in the late 1980s in the Australian school system for students to leave before they completed high school to get a job or apprenticeship in the trade industry; I was one of those young people who left school at 16 years of age to discover my future goals. However, my first day at work overwhelmed me. It was literally sweltering physical work around the bakers' ovens baking bread – not to mention the five p.m. to one a.m. nightshift. It was physically daunting for me as a young person still finding his way in the world. In a matter of days, I soon discovered there was no point trying to build relationships with my co-workers. Most of the workers got angry with me when I did something incorrectly as a first timer. Some of the workers thrived on bullying me with power and words because of their higher position in the company. They seemed proud and bullied me no matter how I felt or how it affected my performance!

I recall trying to toughen up as a young man, brushing off their sarcastic remarks. I often smiled or laughed back at their faces as they continued the bullying and harassment. I remember workers often chatting and joking, which I accepted as a joke about what they termed "mate ship initiation." They often curtailed when I spoke back "to why do such silly thing?" then professed that every apprentice has gone through this initiation process. I was amazed when they brought this subject up!

At work embarked as a good night went well. While working at the bakery the darkest night of my job life set out to transform me in how I would see life and people around me over time. Once we finished production, we would usually start cleaning until next shift would take over from us. Without warning, four to six men workers against one altogether grabbed me – how cowardly! On average most of the workers were at least 10 – 15 years older than me.

I will never forget the feeling of the deranged darkness swallowed me up swiftly. At the time, I felt like how water drains its way down the plughole! I screamed, yelled and swore at those assaulting older men to let me go but they continued to force me to the ground. It felt like my whole world or any thought of its existence had all frozen in time and I had no control over what was taking place!

It happened so quickly I was trying to break free from the forceful grip on me. In that moment, they threatened me to make things worse if I would not let them do what they planned, in order to be part of their own working organization!

Even tho the men were stronger than me I did not give up when they pinned me to the ground. They pulled down my pants, I tried to kick them off yet but they kept pouring a thick syrupy mixture of bread making ingredients all over my private parts and legs helplessly with force.

After my harassment from those men was finally ended they let me go because they got what they wanted, even tho they freed me. I tried not to cry. I ran but found it hard to put my pants on because of the sticky syrups! I shamefully made my way back to the locker room. Some of the female staff and management observed me but they acted like it was a joke.

At the end of my three months probationary period, "I was told I was unsuitable for nightshifts". In contrast, I have been a shift-worker for over 23 years. I've learned to FORGIVE them all.

Sixteen Inspirational Compass Guide:

1. Speak up and try to share your bullied experience with others that you trust especially if you don't have family support or they have lack of understanding which may be due to lack of education, generational gap or social awareness on their part. Otherwise, report it to authorities.

2. Master the art of forgiving those who have harmed you verbally, spiritually, physically or holistically. Your abundance growth is vital despite the uninvited scenarios to keep you growing robustly.

96

3. Fear not and explore your boundaries. Unearth hidden gems to unveil new perspectives connecting the dots. My life experiences beside what I partly shared with you inspired me courageously when I realized there are many victims of bullying, physical abuse, emotional wounds and cyber-bullying these days.

4. Believe in what you can do towards your dreams no matter what episodes ahead of you and use them as your wings to mount from within yourself.

5. Be the VICTOR from those coward bullies! Connect and surround yourself with friendly like-minded people, mentors, coaches and counsellors who will always empower you towards enlarging your passion, dream and vision.

6. Reframe your life situations and life events to align your values with healthy relationships. Imagine your ability to identify the unlabelled opportunity rather than overlooking any barren narrow road.

7. Flourish in those moments of relationships with your family and friend circles, whom you have learned to trust and who inspired you. Apply the practice of timeout from all the stressful distractions from your dreams and goals for at least one day per week or so.

8. You are born to WIN life's battle each day by the great Creator's amazing grace! When there is growth reaching towards your goals, you are in your compass zone trailblazing on your journey.

9. Learn to sustain your solitary journey at the present listening to our Divine given intuition. Discern the traveller's path of your inner intuition compass circumnavigating in the daily events of life.

10. Cultivate the art of listening and seeking wisdom, insightful books, articles and the Creator's nature around us.

11. Own the keys to your kingship mindset. Believe they are like king and queen. Learn to rule them by taking ownership you choose from each key rather than letting others choose for you.

12. Be confident. Engage and comprehend nonverbal communication with people in your social connections.

13. You are MIRACLE from your mother's womb! Your unique crafted life story exists to unleash within you.

14. You are INSPIRATIONAL, dare to pursue!

15. You are the MASTERPIECE! You are GREATER than your challenges when you look back at them!

16. You are the key to your successful journey; it is not all about the destination but the experiences in life-travel that count.

I hope that as you travel along the rough paths, you will define the greatest strengths within you to survive the unforeseen life-travel experiences ahead.

Monica Kunzekweguta

Monica Kunzekweguta is International Author, Certified Life Coach, Motivational Speaker, Owner and CEO at Dream to Action Coaching. Monica is the Project Founder of Inspiration for Kids International.

After obtaining her Degree in Sociology in 1993 she moved to the United Kingdom where she worked as a Manager in the Mental Health sector for over fourteen years; her experience in the Care Sector in general spans over a period of 20 years. She completed self-development and leadership courses; she obtained her Coaching Credentials through Coaching Cognition and is currently doing a Master's Degree in Management. When she is not coaching or supporting her various projects she enjoys watching documentaries, investigative programs and loves to travel.

Contact me:

www.dreamtoactioncoaching.com

🅢 monacun

✉ mkkunze@yahoo.co.uk

𝐟 facebook.com/Monica.Kunzekweguta

🐦 twitter.com/@mona_kunze

CHAPTER 15

I AM THE PRINCESS WHO ESCAPED FROM THE KIDNAPPING ZONE!

By Monica Kunzekweguta

I wasn't being a rebellious child, growing up in Makoni, Zimbabwe. My father overlooked the fact that he had already planted a seed – to quest for success, to be the best and to excel. Whenever I brought home my school report he looked at it meticulously, and we discussed areas which needed improving. He usually asked, "What is going on with your Maths and Geography my girl?" I would give the usual excuses. He always encouraged me to do my best. Our relationship was amazing.

At the age of seven I came home with an impressive report, first position. My father was excited; he bought me a Student's Companion and an English dictionary. I was thrilled – from that I got the message that education was important and if I did well, I would be rewarded.

Ten years later I completed my "O" levels. A serious conflict of interest emerged between the Social Community my father followed and his values. The Social Community did not encourage educating girls beyond primary school; being able to read and write was sufficient. This was a real test to someone who gave up his own studies to help raise his siblings; when I came along some of my uncles were graduates.

The pressure from the community to pull me out of school intensified. This must have been torture for my father. Girls were expected to marry young, and I was getting too old. Men in their forties used to turn up at my boarding school asking for a date when I was a teenager. This was emotionally unbearable and embarrassing. The fear of being kidnapped was real; it was a method used on girls who did not cooperate. I was too embarrassed to tell the officials. This went on for four years. Despite all that, I managed to qualify for "A" levels.

I was told I could not continue with my studies. The atmosphere in the house was somber. After a long discussion I realized that father was not going to budge. That night I cried myself to sleep. I knew that this time things were different, and I needed to act fast.

The next day I was sent to our neighbor's for an iron. A woman greeted me and gave me a mat to sit on. Her husband in his early fifties came into the hut, the wife left immediately. He sang praises for wife then said, "Come and look after each other." I was shocked, but remained calm. I replied, "Let me think about it." His wife came back, gave me the iron and I left.

I had flashbacks; two years earlier at a conference. During the service all girls sat in the front row, followed by young mothers, and elderly women sat at the back. The men's seating arrangement was opposite us. I sat facing one of the prominent leaders. I felt uncomfortable because he kept staring at me. Later, six girls were chosen to fetch water for his wives. Balancing buckets of 20 liters of water on our heads, we walked past the tent where he was relaxing. A few minutes later, two men followed me and told me their leader got a prophecy that I should marry him. They failed to convince me. Their next option was to kidnap me. I had to do something fast, I was desperate. If a girl disappeared, she couldn't go back home, resulting in forced marriage. My friend was already married. She introduced me to her brother-in-law. I used that opportunity to my advantage; I told him, I wanted us to be friends first, he agreed.

I tried going to sleep early but was told to go and socialize. I wore my garment covering my dress; I used my white scarf as a burka to cover my face. I knew that his men would come out in droves looking for me. With nowhere to hide, I went back to our tent, took my six month old half-brother and carried him on my back to blend in with the young mothers. No one approached a married woman, so that way I was safe. My friends promised to protect me. The three of us spent time together walking and chatting; I walked in the middle.

Several men walked in pairs looking for me; they carried torches and sticks. They were determined, asking everyone if they had seen me, they gave a detailed description. I removed my glasses and remained quiet while my friends did the talking. My heart was in my mouth. I went back to our tent around 11:50 p.m. The baby was still sleeping; he had just saved my life. I slept next to him. I could not believe what had happened.

Sunday morning I saw two of the bodyguards. I smiled and winked at them, feeling relieved and excited to go home. To me, daylight represented Hope, Focus, Direction, Determination and Reassurance. I knew I was okay.

I vowed never to set foot in the kidnapping zone again.

Early on Thursday, father accompanied me to the bus stop. It was dark and cold. As we walked I wiped away my tears; I was about to betray my Hero and Mentor. I hid my emotions and managed to chat, disguising the anguish I was going through. Sitting on the bus I waved good-bye until he was out of sight.

I travelled to another village to deliver some money. I cut all my hair; I packed my bag as if I was getting ready for conference, I decided to carry some cash on me always.

The next day I said good-bye and hitchhiked to Harare. I had never done this, and I was scared. My body felt numb, I had experienced too much emotional rollercoaster for many days. I went to Athlone to my maternal grandparents. I didn't want to give up on my dreams. So I did my "A" levels and completed my Degree. The bond between my father and me has healed and is now very strong.

DEAR FRIEND

At the age of seventeen I took this bold decision to leave home. At my tender age of fifteen I faced so many challenges, some of which started when I was even younger, but I did not leave it to someone else to save me. I took the plunge and stepped into the unknown. I want you to know right now that whatever your age, it's not too late to reinvent yourself. No matter how traumatic your past, how devastating your situation is, or how poor your upbringing, you are able to move forward beyond the struggle, beyond survival and thrive.

Make a conscious decision to change your emotions, by changing your thoughts about events which are affecting you or have affected you, leaving you without confidence and hope. Focus on your dreams; focus on your goals and the desired results. This will encourage your subconscious mind to look for solutions to your problems even when you are asleep.

As early as age eleven I already knew what I wanted. I realized that the social community my family belonged to did not support my dreams and my goals in many ways. As a girl I was not supported to continue with my education beyond primary school level. I wanted a better life for myself, and that is what I focused on. When I was fifteen years old I crafted my way out of a possible kidnap. I avoided getting married with nothing to my name. My final plunge came when I was seventeen; I made this decision because I knew that I needed to own my life. I took charge. You can do the same and be in control. Your situation could be worse than what I went through, but you have to do something to change your direction. Have clarity in your mind, what is it you want to enable your subconscious mind to work out or to help solve. Just map out your way to achieving your goals, and live the life you want.

Start right now, make small steps. Focus on you, gain new skills and discover new conversations, these must happen within you before you share with others. Choose to surround yourself with "can do" people who have got a positive outlook on life.

Find your passion and make it your mission to do it to the best of your ability. You might still be experiencing some hardships, but the moment you get to decide what you love, time flies. In the meantime you will be gaining Experience, Confidence, Self-esteem, Dignity, Integrity, Respect and Self-worth. This is what we thrive on; to do something that resonates with our hearts. Do not allow fear to paralyze you, ask yourself, "What is the worst that could happen?"

This will not happen overnight, it takes time, sometimes years, but if you do not take that first step, you will remain in the same position.

Stop looking for approval! You cannot afford to sleepwalk through life.

Ronald Goudreault

Ron is an international author, motivational speaker, business coach/ consultant and trainer. He also held a highly sought position as a former Vice President with Primerica for 7 years. As the former Branch Manager there, he hired and trained many leaders into expanding and opening their own Financial Services Business. He is a father of a 15 year old son whom he enjoys spending quality time with. Ron has a genuine zest for life. He aspires to encourage and motivate others, awakening them to find purpose in their life and discover their own zest for living!

www.rongoudreault.com

🅢 **rgconsulting77**

✉ **ron@rongoudreault.com**

❶ **facebook.com/Health2Wealth4every1**

🐦 **twitter.com/HC4every1**

CHAPTER 16

I HAVE CHOSEN TO DIG MYSELF OUT OF MY DIAGNOSIS

By Ronald Goudreault

Thanking life's natural healing will, I dedicate these words to my miracle son. Years ago I worked myself to exhaustion, creating a life of turmoil. I felt the world crumbling around me in the abyss of darkness. In autumn 2013 I altered my path to ultimately discover a gift that radically transformed my life – and will yours as well.

Who really knows when their last breath will be? We are all born authentic, yet most die as a copy of someone else. This is why I intend to consciously live and presently be attentive to what matters most, that which moves me profoundly, my inner and outer purpose.

I grew up as the youngest in a French Canadian family of 10 kids. I was ashamed of my slim bony physique, and in fear of being laughed at, humiliated, I kept hiding my long skinny toes in the sand when I went swimming. I competed to feel valued by my twin brother, but consistently got lower scores in school and sports. Due to insulting comments for being in an all-girl choir as a child, I buried or resisted my passion for singing and acting. From that point on, I unconsciously started following other people's footsteps instead of my own.

Conditioned to follow my father's dream, I played competitive hockey and fit in well with my twin. I received scholarship applications from Dalhousie and Ohio Universities ranking 34th in OHL goaltending draft picks. With great mentors in the work force I fortunately always achieved leadership positions within companies by helping everyone excel at their own positions. I stayed actively involved in sports of all kinds and felt healthy as a result of it. Being an entrepreneur at age 27 gave me the privilege to attract and develop many great leaders as a Vice President in a Fortune 500 subsidiary company. In a different industry at age 45, I overwhelmed myself as an operation's consultant, with my eyes set on becoming the next General Manager. I literally brought myself to my knees and felt the weight of a mountain crush me when doctors told me this shocking news, "Mr. Goudreault, your muscle fibers are melting and will never come back."

ZAP!!! A lightning bolt paralyzed me that day. This degenerative diagnosis terrified me and I had been keeping these terrors to myself until discovering this universal gift that I will soon reveal. This unexpected adversity started to control me by putting resistance in my mind racing with insecurity, fear, doubt, shame, nuisance, anger, inferiority, sadness, loneliness and confusion to name a few.

At first I sabotaged myself. "Why me? Where have I gone wrong to deserve this? I'm already skinny enough as it is. Now I'm afraid of becoming a breathing skeleton in a wheelchair or trapped in bed for whatever life I have left. What if my heart muscle weakens too and fails me? Could this be why I get pain in my left bicep when I walk more than a couple hundred feet? I feel so crippled, the last thing I want is to be a burden for somebody else."

Then I went through an anger phase. Why am I told by medical professionals that there are no known cures for Muscular Dystrophy when undisclosed associations raised over $2.5 billion since inception? I got frustrated with humanity allowing our own kind to be misled into being experimental subjects and commodities for culprits in a world controlled by greed and power. I became disillusioned, not knowing and wondering where I belonged.

In autumn 2013 as I'm strenuously attempting to stumble my fastest with the strength of an eight year old, with my left toe knuckles paralyzed, BOOM – a thunder blow of shivers blasted down my spine. My 15 year old son casually coasting alongside of me stared right through my eyes and awakened me, "Dad your face is so skinny. I'm afraid you are going to die soon."

I was already devastated for not having the strength to play physical sports with him and felt somewhat inferior, kind of like a failure for not being active or up to par anymore. Talk about a good reason to find purpose in my life as I willed myself to be triumphant in telling the truth without scaring him with perceivable misleading words.

Precisely at that moment I chose being internally strong again, wanting to let it go. Often crying in search for answers and comfort, I started meditating to soothe my confusion. I spent six months by the water in a natural environment, basically disconnecting from the world – revitalizing my cells and allowing my body to find its own healing path. In the process I've learned to never lose myself again to satisfy my mind's perception of success but to always allow self-discovery to manifest its own free will blissfully.

I have been blessed but am now more grateful than ever, for the gift of life in every experience revealing its truth to me. The true gift is life's breath in me regardless of being hospitalized at birth for being critically ill, traumatized as a child by my father's addictive drinking, disturbed in my twenties by my schizophrenic nephew taking his life. I've been saddened by my father's aneurysm causing death, scared in my early thirties by a rare degenerative disease taking my sister's life and disabling another sister. I was appalled in my late thirties by systems pushing drugs on my ADHD son for curriculum acceptance and now tested in my forties by a diagnosis bringing my physical strength to that of a child and threatening two of my older sisters.

Every second now, I'm creating an improved authentic version of myself by exploring my true essence and deliberately digging myself out of my diagnosis. Since my son awakened me, I went from 5 minutes soft trampoline bounce to 12 minutes full bounce daily, from 15 second plank to 5 min plank daily and from 2 sets of 6 modified pushups to 3 sets of 10 standard pushups.

Ron's Personal Perspective:

My dearest reader, I am no doctor or medical specialist but as a breathing testimony of life's miracle, I had the privilege of helping many people find inner truth – also to become fulfilled in their life. In doing so, experience has taught me to learn from and recognize how special you are.

- Please do not allow the physical world to mold you into something you are not. If you have fallen prey to identifying with any perceptions created in the mind such as thoughts, beliefs, emotions and diagnosis, rejoice as they do not define you. I choose not to allow my diagnosis or my family's medical history define me, because I am the programmer of my own genetics.

- What defines you is universal truth, life creating its own existence through your breath, visually assessing its evolution through your mind. You are life unfolding itself with an awareness and ability to observe, learn and fulfill your true essence. I now, more than ever, feel the universe expanding itself through me, as I embrace every experience in applying the lessons resonating with my internal bliss.

- Everything that relates to the physical world perceived in your mind occurs for you to be a student of (not the identity of), as lessons qualifying you towards your true higher evolutionary self. That is why I challenge myself to deliberately always give birth to innovative intuitive solutions in every present moment.

- Your physical perception mirrors your personal love frequency which is tuned by an ACCEPTANCE or RESISTANCE dial regulating the data programmed in your mind's software since your creation. I feel strongly about this, because the more I resonate with unconditional acceptance of experiences the more alive I feel, since love harmonizes my mind.

- Acceptance means you know not being the identity your mind perceives. Therefore, exercise your own right to delete what no longer serves you and upload new data in favor of your bliss. I observe experiences to constantly recreate myself because my senses confirm what was has now become old news.

- Resistance means you believe being the identity your mind perceives. Therefore, resist improving the perceptive reality of yourself. I refuse to be realistic because it builds resistance in my universe that is naturally meant to be abundant in all aspects.

You are greater than your mind's perception which is the processing department of all chosen experiences. For you to embrace everything about yourself, you need to discover how to become the best version of you. Picture your beliefs, thoughts, emotions and diagnosis as clouds passing beneath you while you are the infinite sky. Drift to a place of acceptance as you now realize no identity in the physical world can be placed upon you, as you are beyond every perception created in your mind. Love yourself – miraculous healing soul that you are. Apologize internally for resisting your own self-discovery. Forgive yourself for your realistic human ways. Thank yourself for the life that you are and the deliberate creator you set forth here to be.

Olive Walters

Olive is a Law of Attraction Practitioner, Trainer, Speaker, Realtor and CEO and owner of Trecourt Virtual Services Inc. She is very passionate about the fact that she can utilize the Law of Attraction to literally create the life that she desires. She enjoys inspiring others and teaching them how to use it to create abundance and peace in their own lives.

Olive is a mother, grandmother and lover of life. With love, everything is possible.

- IamOliveWalters@gmail.com
- facebook.com/olive.walters.90
- @owalters
- pinterest.com/OliveWalters
- ca.linkedin.com/in/olivewalters

CHAPTER 17

MY RELATIONSHIP WAS RED FLAGGED!

By Olive Walters

There seems to be a defining moment in one's life that makes such an immense impact, shakes you up and puts you on a trajectory that you might not otherwise have thought of. It is up to you to follow that path where it may lead you. ~ *Olive Walters*

The crash of broken glass pierced through the silence, startling me from my sleep. Heavy footsteps stomped towards my bedroom. I sat up, strained to focus on the figure who was now standing at the foot of the bed. It was then that I saw my estranged ex-boyfriend holding a knife. He dragged me out of the bedroom. He punched me repeatedly and slammed me into a glass coffee table which shattered under my weight. At one point he had me on the ground with his knee in my chest pinning me down. I had my hands wrapped around his grip on the knife and was using every bit of my strength to keep the knife from plunging into my chest. Horrible thoughts flooded through my mind of what would happen if I ran out of strength. Suddenly I heard my nine year old daughter scream at him "Don't kill mommy!" That startled him; he pulled away and yelled at her to go back to her room. The one thing that he kept saying over and over was "Neither one of us are leaving here alive".

I finally managed to escape and ran from the house with him close behind me. There was a police station a couple of streets away that I thought I could run to, but the combined effects of the beating, my fear and loss of control threw me into a state of panic. In my exhaustion I only made it a few houses away. I ran to a neighbour's and started banging on the heavy solid oak door screaming for help. Finally after what seemed like an eternity, the owners of the house opened the door and were startled to see me bleeding, half-naked at their doorstep at 2:30am. I knew at that moment that someone was looking over me.

Months later I could still remember thinking that nothing could have prepared me for the flood of emotions that followed that experience. Feelings ranging from shame, embarrassment, fear, hatred towards him, hatred towards myself, unworthiness, the list goes on. I felt so embarrassed and ashamed that someone who I cared for wanted me dead. I knew I didn't have the best track record in past relationships but I kept asking myself "Am I so repulsive that emotional, psychological and physical abuse was not enough, death was what I deserved?" I felt that everyone who knew about the incident also knew that I was garbage. Intellectually I knew that his actions were not my fault, but I still tried to figure out what I did to deserve that kind of treatment. I couldn't think of anything. I just felt that I wasn't good enough, pretty enough and definitely not worthy of love. Prior to this, after each failed relationship I went through a mourning period where I scolded myself for being stupid to believe that I was worthy of love. I told myself that some people were meant to be loved and others were not...I was in the latter group. After surviving the brutal ordeal I was even more convinced that I was not one of those lucky ones who were destined to be loved.

In the months that followed, I strived to appear like everything was normal in my world but inside I was struggling. I had nightmares every night for about year. I would see him standing at the bus stop or at the subway station waiting for me. I would have terrors of other men holding me from behind so that he could have better access to hurt me. It was as if I was trapped. I tried many ways to distract myself. I was even obsessed with watching a popular television show about inmates living in a very violent jail. I would imagine it was him getting raped, beat up, fed ground-up glass and killed. It kind of made me feel better if you can believe that. Yep it was a dark time. It was my strange way of coping and surviving. I finally stopped watching it when a friend asked me why I was torturing myself like that. That was a major shift in my perspective. I Woke Up and realized it wasn't healthy. It got to the point where I couldn't stomach it anymore. I didn't want to attract those feelings much less any of those experiences.

Physically, my body was a mess. I didn't sleep more than a few hours each night and was probably underweight given that I am small framed. I felt like I was in physical pain for months, I don't know if I was just healing very slowly from the trauma or if it was more emotionally based. My menstrual cycle even stopped for 6 months. I was afraid all the time, whether I was on the way to or from work and definitely at home especially if my brother wasn't there. I avoided dating like the plague.

I was very fortunate though to have the people that I did in my life at the time. My boss demanded the day after the ordeal that I go into a local shelter. It was there that I got my first counseling sessions. It helped me to break off some limiting beliefs that I had embraced for so long. From there I was encouraged to seek out my support services at my place of employment and I was able to make some major shifts on my path to healing.

I had to learn to forgive myself. For what you may ask? For not listening to my inner voice. I ignored all the little signs in the beginning that told me that this relationship was not healthy. Based on my previous unhealthy relationships I didn't want to bring the wrong-doings of the last person into the new relationship…I was so worried about blaming him for things that the last guy did, that I overlooked crap that I shouldn't have. My internal protective mechanism was picking up on things but I didn't want to process them. We all have amazing inner voices. We should start listening to them. My insecurities kept me from acting on the information that I was refusing to process, from acting on what I knew I should be doing, if not for myself, then at least for my kids. I had to learn to keep forgiving myself for ignoring the signs that were actually red flags.

It wasn't an overnight process. It took years to heal from this and learn to love myself. With support from friends and loved ones especially my children I am at a good place in my life.

RELATIONSHIP RED FLAGS

- Red Flag 1. – *Alcohol and Substance Abuse* – Please don't ignore this or make excuses for it. I made this mistake. At the court hearing he said the night he broke into my home with the knife he had drank a case of beer and it gave him the "liquid courage" he needed. **Wake up!**

- Red Flag 2. – *Animosity, Anger or Racism towards Others.* – If your partner has a strong hatred for groups of people, that is a major indication of turmoil in their life. How can they have capacity to love you if they have hate for others that they do not even know? **Wake up!**

- Red Flag 3. – *Blaming Others* – The man that I was involved with blamed his mother, grandmother, sister and ex-wife for all the pain in his life. He took no responsibility for any of his actions. As far as he was concerned, they were the cause of any wrong-doing on his part. **Wake up!**

- Red Flag 4. – *Manipulative and Controlling* – Many abusive partners use control tactics that sound like "If you love me you will…" I heard this often. The last straw was when he said "If you don't take me back I will kill myself." Please don't wait for it to get that far. This is not a normal healthy way to communicate with someone you love. It's a form of abuse. **Wake up!**

- Red Flag 5 – *History of Damaged Relationships* – You will pick up on your partner's subtle or extreme patterns of unhealthy damaged relationships. This could be with their family or others, for example neighbors, co-workers, classmates. Please don't ignore this. These people don't seem to have the capacity to form caring, productive and positive relationships. **Wake up!**

Dear friend, if my story resonates with you, I encourage you to use this phrase that I often use to reset my perspective. Repeat it softly to yourself when needed as often as you need.

I love you. I'm sorry. Please forgive me. Thank you.

Viviana Andrew

Viviana Andrew is a Certified Coach, an Online Business Consultant, a Law of Attraction Practitioner and an International Bestselling Author along with 30 mentors in the book "Living Without Limitations – 30 Mentors to Rock Your World." She was born in Indonesia and currently resides in Malaysia. Her strength is in networking and online marketing. She has built an extensive network through her online business and overcame her limiting belief by embracing an empowering belief, "I believe in success." Her mission is empowering solo entrepreneurs to create their own success and build an online business with passion, clarity and uniqueness.

www.vivianaandrew.com

 facebook.com/VivianaCoaching

 twitter.com/coach_viviana

 youtube.com/viviwid09

 linkedin.com/profile/in/viviana

CHAPTER 18

THE POWER OF UNCONDITIONAL LOVE HELPS ME TRANSFORM MY REJECTIONS AND INSPIRE MY LIFE

By Viviana Andrew

"You are just a girl from the small town [Tuban]," said my cousins, who often mocked and laughed at me when we played together when we were young. I was born and raised in a small coastal town of Tuban, Indonesia. So, I begged my parents to let me study in the big city of Surabaya, Indonesia even if it meant living apart from them. I loved the glamour of the city life, and it seemed to me at that time that city kids were smarter too. True, study was hard and living apart from my parents was even harder. I had to live with my relatives with four kids. My uncle and my aunt were not well off. I heard them complain about money almost every day. I learned the hard life at the age 10.

Looking back, I am surprised that I managed to live through the ordeal. Maybe it was because I wanted to be on par with kids in the city so much more. I never complained to my parents about having made the choice I wanted. I strove hard to prove to others that I could be more than just average. I wanted acknowledgement. The reason why I was willing to learn more and took up challenges was because I wanted to be treated like other seemingly well-to-do kids.

When I was in high school, the English club teacher expected us to raise funds for our trip, so we would not need to ask for money from our parents. I recalled the constant bickering between my aunt and uncle about how hard it was for them to earn money. I did not like selling to my family and friends. Selling made me feel like asking people for their money.

I thought of selling things to my relatives to do my part. I could still remember vividly my experience of trying to sell to my uncle's fiancée. She appeared to be a nice person to everybody, to my parents and my uncle. One day, when I went to her house alone, she started treating me like a pest. She scolded me for taking up her precious time, but she went on and on to lecture me. I remembered holding back my tears. When I finally walked out from her gate, I broke down in tears. I found out then how a person could be nice and yet so harsh.

Ever since then, I got nervous when it came to selling. I avoided courses that have to do with selling and chose to study engineering instead. When I started working, I shied away from marketing. Even then, I could not avoid it for long because one of the training requirements in my company was to sell, and I dreaded it and expected to fail badly. True, what I thought would happen did happen. I felt embarrassed – I was already an adult and I was the head of my department. I cried for the second time. The rejection that started in my childhood seemed to follow me to my teenage years and young adulthood.

I always tell myself that it is not good to ignore or bottle up bad feelings in my life. I have learned over the years that if I hide those feelings, it will seep into my subconscious mind. They will turn into my limiting beliefs and stop me from taking positive actions in my life.

I remember experiencing my first reconciliation at a healing retreat. I was then a student in the university (UPN Veteran, Surabaya, Indonesia). It was a weekend retreat program for the youth. The program helped me look back into my life and heal the relationship problems I had in the past. I was able to love my parents again, to forgive my aunt and to reconcile my relationships with the people around me. I was required to send letters of gratitude to the people that I loved and connected to. People who received my letters of gratitude – my father, my mother and my aunt – were shocked and moved to tears after reading my deepest sincere words of appreciation and apology.

I always thought my parents were mean to me and thought that they did not love or accept me when they labeled me a naughty or rebellious child. I assumed that I behaved unacceptably, because I

119

believed my mother and grandmother played favorite to my sister who was smarter and deemed a good girl. I chose to live with my relatives to avoid hearing the word naughty or rebellious from my parents. I have gone through much emotional turmoil to shed my rebellious behavior.

Eventually, I turned into a shy, sensitive but well-behaved young woman. The second healing retreat that I went to was when I had already become a mother to two kids. I joined the program without knowing what it was all about. In that retreat, I discovered that my parents had wanted a baby boy before I was born. When I was small, I was dressed up like a boy and had my hair cut like a boy. I resented my mother and grew close to my father. In the retreat, I asked forgiveness from God and changed my ill feelings towards my mother. My lack of communication was also because I kept all those feelings of resentment within me and thought that nobody loved me. Now that I am a mother, I choose to love my children unconditionally.

If every child or person is accepted and loved unconditionally, they will lead a happy and successful life. They will unconsciously develop their potential to the maximum. Those parents who receive coaching or have self-coaching skills, will become better parents and understand what needs to be done to help their children become more confident and achieve their ambitions in life. And if every child receives coaching at school or at home, she will become a better child, able to manage and understand her emotional well-being.

The Power of Loving Yourself Unconditionally Propels You to Inspire Your Ambition.

The power of love has a big impact on your personal growth. The feelings of rejection and not being loved can lead to self-loathing; you do not care about your life, and you do not like being you. You wonder why your life leads to failure, bad luck and unhappiness. There is a tendency for some people to self-destruct their own life because they no longer love themselves. If you have the feeling that life does not favor you or nobody loves you, I want you to stop and think, whose life will it benefit if you love yourself unconditionally?

There is a power in your mind that you can harness to become the person you think you can be.

- A person who says "I don't deserve to be successful," will not take any action to make himself successful. Nothing he does is an effort to improve himself, and he does not have a positive outlook on his life.

- A person who says "I deserve to be successful," will constantly strive to be successful. He ignites his self-belief by taking positive actions in his life.

You can transform the power of loving yourself unconditionally into a power to inspire your ambition.

- If you learn to love yourself, you will enjoy living from moment to moment. Everyone is born special. Know yourself and be grateful for what you have. Take a look at your body, your health, your talents/strengths and what you can do. Take a look at your weaknesses, how you can improve them to become your strengths. If you have self-awareness, you believe you can do more to inspire your ambition. You develop yourself more because you love yourself, and you take actions to achieve your ambition.

- If you love yourself, you can build good relationships with others. Learn to love the other person first by greeting, giving attention, saying, "Hello. How are you?" Give your love first instead of expecting to be loved. When you give, you feel a lot better about yourself and people reciprocate. Your ambition is not only about personal achievement. If it is connected to other people, your act of giving will certainly help you and others to succeed.

- Find support from the community and a coach. Everyone needs a listener. If you have a bottled up negative emotion, it can affect your behavior. If you want to keep your ambition inspired, you need to have an accountability partner as in a coach or mastermind group.

The power of loving yourself unconditionally will benefit you. You will be propelled to inspire your ambition more when you love yourself without conditions. There are endless possibilities that you can achieve with your life. And life is not just about you, as you are connected to other people. Your family and the people around you will benefit from your happiness.

Patrick Hayden

Patrick Hayden is a personal Life Mentor, a Life Coach with a difference, an Inventor and an International Bestselling Author in the book "Living Without Limitations – 30 Mentors to Rock Your World."

His personal drive within his heart is to help others overcome their brickage and blockage beliefs and enhance their lives to the success they deserve.

Married for 28 years to his beautiful wife Cora, who has stood by him through thick and thin, he has three wonderful sons, and in June 2014 he will be a grandfather.

He is now enjoying living life without limits.

www.thegreatlightconnections.com

✉ patohayden@gmail.com

⌾ facebook.com/patrick.hayden.96

⌾ twitter.com/PatoHaydo

⌾ pinterest.com/togethers/pins

CHAPTER 19

I BROKE THROUGH THE WALL OF DOUBT
By Patrick Hayden

Let me start this chapter by saying thanks to a woman who saw something in my words and believed I had something to share with the World. Thank you so much, Anita Sechesky; you came into my life after I had reached rock bottom. At that time I laid the new foundation for myself, giving me the spark to create light and show the World my gift. We will remain connected in the spirit of truths.

As a professional Life Coach, the discovery of breaking through the Wall of Doubt while conquering bipolar was no easy challenge but in all fairness, I had many tools. I was also working with my brother and son in our innovation company; this gave me a great foundation.

What is the Wall of Doubt? Where did it come from? How can we demolish it? Many people on the Earth experience self-sabotage by the Wall of Doubt; they feel trapped inside themselves, and thus live a poor quality of life. I can say this because I was once in those shoes.

First, let me explain to you what the Wall of Doubt is. The Wall of Doubt is constructed by you and by the influences you receive from others – meaning adults, teachers, family and friends. Our mind has two sides, the conscious side, which is the side that wants things and the subconscious, which is the side that is connected to your spirit and abundance. As newborns our minds are pure and the two minds are connected; but as we ask questions we start to construct the Wall of Doubt between the two minds. There are two types of belief blocks that we place in the Wall of Doubt, one is brickage-beliefs, which are small beliefs and the other is blockage-beliefs, which are convictions.

These beliefs are placed in the Wall of Doubt by the questions we ask, so some of them are wrongly placed beliefs and hold us back from our true self. This self-sabotage restricts our true growth, as we live most of our lives in the conscious mind.

I was in my early 40s when I fell ill with a condition called bipolar. I believed that this was brought on by being too nice and placing my trust in the answers of others. I would do anything for others; my biggest problem was that I could not say NO to people. I would often put myself out for others; this habit became so ingrained in me that it was impossible for me to say no. People and friends took huge advantage of my weakness, but what was happening to me was that my Wall of Doubt was building hugely between the two minds, my doubt was becoming super powerful against me; this was the main cause of my bipolar.

While building the Wall of Doubt, I noticed when you ask a person a question, they love to answer it. It's the feeling of importance that they are after, even if their answer to you only has partial truth. On the discovery of this, I made a rule to myself; any questions that I need answers to, I would seek professional advice. Remember, if I can teach you anything from this chapter, please let it be this: when seeking advice, ask only people who are qualified enough to give such advice, for it should only be professional advice that you use to build the new Doors to Success.

While lying in bed at night, my thoughts would often race; it was a horrible feeling. Thoughts from every story in my life, thoughts like outstanding bills, career, relationships and from my past. They would enter my mind and speed through the stories. I had no control over what thoughts came in or what stories I could revisit. These thought patterns would happen for long periods of time and I was exhausted; I never got much sleep. These patterns were compelling my bipolar. My emotions and feelings were flying up and down in seconds, the butterflies in my tummy were so intense and the sad depressed feelings of complete emptiness and loneliness were unbearable.

Here's how I broke through the Wall of Doubt:

One day I was telling my brother and son, whom I have an innovation business with, about the racing thoughts I was having. My brother said "Paddy, when the thoughts start racing, shout out loud in your own mind, 'STOP!'" The next time the racing thoughts showed up, I remembered the technique my brother told me, I used it and it worked, so I keep using it each time and now they are GONE, some years since.

Another discovery was brought to me by my son – exercising peace of mind. An exercise to prove to myself that I'm in control of my thoughts. When I go for a walk with my little dog I say to myself, "I'm going to clear my head from thoughts," so I can decide when. What I do is, I say to myself, "At this next street lamp, I'm not going to think about anything at all and I'm going to clear my thoughts until I reach the next street lamp." On my first attempt, it lasted two seconds, then I tried again and it was for five seconds, I thought that this was going to be impossible but I practiced and practiced, now I can tell you, it's a wonderful gift from God and the control and peace of mind is beautiful.

The last of the three things is, I sought only advice from competent professionals. I can't emphasize this enough; remember the answers from others built the Wall of Doubt. There is a God – anytime I want anything in my life, I ask the Universe and I always receive. Mind you, I do allow time to receive and funny as it may seem, it always comes back at the right moment.

The only thing holding you back from success is your Wall of Doubt, though most of you will disagree and tell me that it is others or outside circumstances that hold you back. Let me tell you when you try to achieve something new, your ego – the voice in your head – will make plenty of excuses as to why you will not be able to achieve the new idea; excuses like you don't have the money or the time, or you are not skilled enough. The ego lives in your stories in the Wall of Doubt between the two minds, the conscious mind and the subconscious mind; the ego will give its life to hold you prisoner in the conscious mind. Its life by the way is the stories in the brickage-beliefs and the blockage-beliefs that lie in the Wall of Doubt. The reason you dwell in your past memories/stories is the work of your ego; the ego grows stronger when it has control over you.

How does the ego get stronger in you? Every time you try something new and fail, the Wall of Doubt grows stronger. The ego will say things to you like, I had a feeling that would not work, or you can try it again sometime. The ego knows you inside out and it works on your downfall; it is sly and slippery – it is clever – and it will try every trick in the book to defeat you. Here is a simple task for you to try, STOP THINKING, clear your mind of everything for 20 seconds; see how hard it is to do. The reason for that is the ego has built itself into the voice of your thoughts and pretends to be you talking to you. The one thing I did to take control of my ego was, I would say things to myself, things like I might try to do this new thing tomorrow or next week. My ego would not know which day I was going to try the new thing, so it could not set the plan for me to fail. Self-sabotage comes from the ego but when it doesn't know your plan it will fail to fail you. The ego is a part of you, but for most it is larger than them. When you keep your plans to your true self, you will be successful, and every time you succeed the ego gets weaker. You should not aim to kill the ego just tame it, so it doesn't have the say in your plans.

Breaking through the Wall of Doubt can be tricky, because the ego does not want to be the underdog. So start by taking out the brickage beliefs, the smaller beliefs in the Wall of Doubt. When you break through the Wall of Doubt, you will enter the subconscious mind where your spirit and abundance lies. Most people call this part of the mind the creative side, connected to God where all ideas come from.

Thank you for reading my chapter. I hope it was useful to you, and I look forward to assisting you sometime soon.

La-toya Fagon

Chef La-toya, born in Canada of Jamaican descent, fell in love with cooking at an early age. She attended George Brown's Chef School and continued to train at a number of top restaurants and hotels throughout Toronto, the Caribbean and Mexico. After gaining years of experience, La-toya's creativity started to flourish and she crafted her own take on "Island Paradise," fusing her cooking style of traditional Caribbean ingredients together with Mediterranean flavors. La-toya tapped into her entrepreneurial spirit, and Twist Catering came to fruition. She uses her passion for food matched with her vibrant and contagious personality to please the palate.

✉ twist@twistcatering.com

ⓕ Twist Catering - La-toya

ⓨ @twistcatering

ⓖ @twistcatering

ⓘ La-toya Fagon

CHAPTER 20

WOMAN WITH A SECRET

By La-toya Fagon

I have a secret.

Have you ever walked with shame? Or have you ever carried embarrassment? What's your secret? A person with shame doesn't hold their head down, they walk with it held high as they carry their shame.

This is my life story; this is how I've chosen to live my life. No matter what has happened in the past, I don't let it define me; I am more than that. Suck it up boo, there are bigger things happening in life than what pain I've gone through. So stop it! Move on, no one wants to hear it, and let's be real – I don't want to tell it.

It's a new day, a new year. Things are going fine; working hard on achieving my goals, striving to be the best, working on being successful. Because if I am not successful then what am I?

I have to keep the smile; I am reliable and people do depend on me. So I always push my feelings aside, however painful. I'll pick myself up, dust my shoulders off and keep doing what I do. I'm a superstar, superwoman under the spotlight.

I have no time to feel emotions, being surrounded by people every day, having lots of friends. Yet not one true friend to share everything with, no one knowing my gloom and despair. Because I've been living with these secrets for so long, it's been impossible to give 100% of me to anyone. I am the master of blocking and tucking anyway anything that will cause an emotional trigger; I've allowed myself to be cold to myself. I'm always having flashes of what went wrong. What could

I have done differently? Holding my shame, because what can I do, I'm the strong one. Nothing can hurt me, nothing bothers me.

No one knows what it's like day in and day out. I wake up, doing what I do best, what I've trained myself to be and do and what people think I am. If my mind wanders, I snap out of it as quickly as possible. I don't allow myself to go down that path, just tuck it and go. No one really knows me. They think they know. But they only know what I tell them and show them.

But that is what makes me a warrior; I can do what I do, day in and day out. I used to shed tears and I don't shed tears anymore even when I am in my darkest moment and all alone. I smile and shine every day, I make people happy. Because of the things that I have been through and am going through, I never break down. I'll never let them know. Thank God, I've never broken down or let myself run with my feelings. If I ever did, I would probably have a mental breakdown or something worse than I myself, much less anyone else, could even recognize. Then this life that I'm working so hard to build would not exist. I wouldn't know how to crawl back out from the despair and the darkness.

Every day is a good day. I practically forget everything that makes me feel anything less than a superstar. I live so positively and I am focused on bringing that positivity out to the world. I'm doing amazing things and want to continue to do amazing things in my life. God is good to me – he always has been; even when I thought I was walking alone in the darkness I've been pulled out. There are way bigger things happening to people, way more serious things. I have a warm home, food, family and friends. The things that I know that are important. And that is what I repeat to myself every day to keep it moving.

But once in a blue moon in that moment of silence, I see darkness – I do remember, and I do feel that pain. But I snap back and say to myself your pain isn't that bad because how else would I tuck it away? But then I think I've just become the master of not feeling the negative. That doesn't mean that I think that I am better than anyone else, I just deal differently than others. I've learned to manage and control emotions that have triggers. It's my life even though many may have tried to crush, destroy, not support me or the dream; I still stand strong.

Now I ask myself, does it ever go away? The answer is no, and it never will because it's all my secrets that I am taking to the grave with me, and it's not just one secret. And there are times that there may have been others involved. But what I've realized is when they move on and I am left with the emotional baggage, it's my problem – my issue – nobody else's. It's seems like it's millions of secrets, and one leads to another which leads to another, which leads to lies on top of lies; and it has manifested into something that I can't control anymore. So the only thing I could do was keep it locked up.

I like being different, I like being unique, I like knowing that I think differently from everyone else. Sometimes when I feel like lying down and giving up, I always hear a little voice from somewhere unknown that tells me to get up! And asks me what are you doing? That voice brings me back. It brings me out of the doom and the gloom. The secrets are just that, they never break me down, they are just secrets – I just keep saying that over and over. They don't define me. I don't let them.

What is a secret anyway? To me it is something that is kept unknown, unheard or unseen by anyone else. It is mine and with that I define me, no one else; and I am ok with that, I love me.

I want everyone to know that if you have a secret, don't feel pressured to speak about it. It's your secret to do what you want with it. Know like I know that it is ok, to hold something and never let it go, as long as you can hold it and it doesn't destroy you. Letting a secret destroy you, destroys the idea of holding it, because we've allowed it to consume us.

I know that I am stronger because of the things that I have gone through in life, the hardships, fears and lowest moments; and still I rise and so will you. We are warriors for pushing through day to day without letting our secrets and fears show to others. We tuck it in and keep moving, and we keep moving with a force that drives us to greatness. We do not accept failure, because by doing so, we accept the fact that we didn't try for happiness, and not trying is something that I cannot live with.

I know that I am not perfect, and that is okay. What is perfect anyway? I've made mistakes, which is a part of life. I use to look at them as failures, but they are not failures – they are experiences that have made me better, and they will make you better too. I learn from every experience and you should too. My mistake or secret does not define who I am as a person. I take accountability for my mistakes. I can't right my wrongs; they are too far gone. But the whole point is, we don't have to right the wrong we just need to accept it and work towards never letting the same mistake or wrong happen again. Acceptance is an amazing trait to hold, allow you to release yourself of shame. I have allowed myself to release the shame.

Whenever you're feeling overwhelmed just say these things to yourself "I will overcome any obstacle in time." "If I can't solve a problem, I am strong enough to accept that. I have overcome many obstacles and difficult times in my life and I know that this may change me or my life, but it will be for the better." "I will find more strength every day to move past things, because I have so much more exploring to do. I am tough and strong and I give thanks and praise for my accomplishments and successes."

Happiness is a state of mind, and I choose to find things in my life to be happy and grateful for. I released what I had no control over, and trusted myself that in time my secrets and mistakes will become a thing of the past. My life is what I make of it, and I choose to make it an amazing and joyful ride. I allow myself to be sad for a moment but not for long, there is not time for sadness. I know I am needed, valued and appreciated by others. I am my own best friend and love myself unconditionally.

Anita Sechesky

Anita is a Registered Nurse, Certified Life Coach, International Best Selling Author, Speaker, Trainer, NLP and LOA Wealth Practitioner, as well as Big Vision Consultant. She studied Marketing at the School of Online Business and completed her Advanced Certificate of Life Coaching at Academy of Coaching Cognition. She is the CEO and Owner of Anita Sechesky – Living Without Limitations. Anita has assisted many people breaking through their own limiting beliefs in life and business. She has two International Best Sellers and is compiling her third anthology "Living Without Limitations – 30 Stories to Love Your World," to be released in 2014.

You can contact Anita at the following:

www.anitasechesky.com

🆂 anita.sechesky

✉ asechesky@hotmail.ca

𝐟 facebook.com/AnitaSechesky

𝐟 facebook.com/asechesky

🐦 @nursie4u

𝓟 pinterest.com/anitasechesky

in ca.linkedin.com/pub/anita-sechesky/3b/111/8b9

CHAPTER 21

THE HUMAN SPIRIT
By Anita Sechesky

The human spirit is so magnificent. It is the connection to the human mind and body and it even has the capacity to connect with other human beings. We can almost feel the emotional pain or trauma another person has lived through. I believe that love is such a powerful energy that it causes our spirits to become connected as one. I am a strong believer that our spirits live forever.

For this chapter, I would like to share my own personal experience when I had lost my first child. My daughter was full-term and she was a perfect baby. There was nothing wrong the entire pregnancy. However, we did lose our beautiful little girl due to unforeseen causes. I had known something was not right and felt it within my spirit. I asked my doctor if I could be induced to have my daughter delivered two weeks early. My obstetrician's office was over two hours away from my home. He decided not to interfere with the natural birth process that was planned since there wasn't any cause for concern at this point. When I went to the Emergency Department in a small northern community I was always told by the nurses that everything was fine, even though my baby's heart rate was lower as compared to earlier assessments in my pregnancy. This occurred before I became a Registered Nurse and disturbed me, as I already had some medical knowledge at the time.

My pregnancy loss with my daughter was the most heartbreaking thing I have endured. No one from the hospital offered any support. Sadly, the loss of my baby was not the first one in this community. I tried to tell the nurses so many times that something was not right, but no one took me seriously. I must have gone to the Emergency Department at least a dozen times and was always told that I was

COMPILED BY **ANITA SECHESKY**

overthinking or something to that effect. The last time I went to Emergency, they staff finally took me seriously and put a stress monitor on me. All the previous times I went in, the stress monitor was being used or I was just sent home. I wasn't even given the option to wait for the monitor for a short duration to confirm my concerns.

As it turned out, my precious baby girl was stillborn and I had to deliver her on a maternity ward during the Christmas holidays, just two days before my own birthday. It was painful to see the other mothers and their live babies.

The night before my induction, my daughter's little baby spirit came to me and before I knew it, I was hovering above looking down at my husband lying next to my lifeless body. I saw how my hands were folded across my pregnant belly with my daughter still within my womb. I remember looking at how beautiful and bright she was and then, just like that, I got caught up in the instantaneous rapture of leaving my physical body. Then as I was travelling upwards into the heavenly realms with my daughter, I remembered what my mom had just moments earlier spoken to me about, and I looked back down at my husband sleeping. She said that I should remember how much he loved me, and that we would have more children one day. The very moment that thought flashed through my mind, I was back inside my physical body and looking at my hands folded in front of me.

This experience left me realizing that death is only a transition and not a physical effort at all. In fact, my experience was completely effortless and merely a shift out of my physical body into my spiritual body. I believe that we already have our spiritual body inside of us and when we no longer need our physical bodies, we simply leave it behind.

However you may want to analyze it, I can say this was a profound and powerful revelation that gave me confirmation of life after death. How amazing to know that we never actually die or lose ourselves, but we are intact in our thoughts even after our physical bodies stop working! This is why I am a strong believer in my Christian faith. I choose to believe that I will be reunited with my loved ones and even embrace my baby girl once more in my arms.

I have learned that our spirit man is the essence of who we are. This concept is so profound that it can help us to become stronger in this life if we allow ourselves to accept that nothing is impossible, and that all is possible if we believe.

Yes, the human spirit is powerful and I can even tell you an experience I had with one of my pets. When our dear family pet died, it was a hard time for all of us, as our doggie girl was part of our family for over 13 years. She was like our first child and she was well loved within our community by our friends and family. I will never forget that following the first Mother's Day service after we had lost our daughter, our pet doggie came into the bedroom and looked at me crying as I was curled up on my bed. She jumped up and snuggled right against my belly, as if someone had coaxed her to do that. She stayed there for a brief moment, jumped down, looked at me, and then walked away. When our beloved pet passed away at my parent's home, it was devastating because we never had a chance to say good-bye to her. The following day, I was sitting in my glider rocking chair just thinking that I never had a chance to tell her how much I loved her. All of a sudden, out of nowhere, I literally felt this amazing rush of energy. It was like a swift breeze. Before I knew it, our dog in her spiritual form was sitting right next to me by my feet. Then automatically I felt my spirit man lean down, pat her, and even say, "Good girl." I couldn't believe this was happening and excitedly told my husband that I got to say goodbye to our pet. He was so happy and never doubted me because of the supernatural experiences I already had.

My reason for sharing these events is to help you realize that our spirit is something that we all contain within us. There is no explaining it. I believe from the time our cells are conceived and start vibrating, we are created out of pure love and positive energy as we are all perfect creations by God within this Universe and all its glory. There is no need to fear the fact that our spirit is something that is unexplained. In fact, I believe in some special way if we embrace our lives differently, we may be exposed to more infinite possibilities that we would never have realized were always around us anyway. Many people already know that GOD is a spirit, as we cannot see HIM yet we believe HE exists around us. Be open minded to what our Creator has created within you. You are unique and wonderfully made. Never doubt the endless possibilities of your human spirit. This life is but a journey and we are all headed in the same direction.

As you already know, my intention for this book is to help you see how we are all connected. We don't have to personally know each other to understand life's hardships, trauma, and pain. Our unity as individuals simply believing in the common good creates a connection within our spirits. Can you imagine so many people across the globe equally realizing the need to reach out and show more empathy, compassion, and love for those around them? The human spirit ignited in love will unite many. God is Love. Have you connected with Him as yet? It's all about relationship, not rituals. Just like any other relationship, start with introducing yourself. HE accepts you just as you are. Maybe it's time you do the same. Healing will become one of the benefits from this relationship. It all starts with you wanting more for yourself. The human spirit is one of the most beautiful gifts we have been given. It has unlimited possibilities.

Many times we may face extreme difficulties in our lives. When all hope is lost, what do you do? Do you have a support system? Not everyone does. It is a sad reality in this big world. Lives are changed instantly as a result of either good or bad experiences. When you carry pain deep within your heart, it affects the vibrancy of your life. Maybe it's time to start associating with positive people. Discover what your life's passions are by searching deep within your soul. You can begin your own healing right now, right where you are.

Rudo Bingepinge-Dzenga

Rudo is an Internationally published Author, Trainer, Inspirational Speaker, Actress. She was 2nd Runner up 2013: Toastmasters Southern Africa International prepared Speech Competitions.

She holds a Sociology Degree, a Diploma in Marketing and a Masters in Business Administration. With over 11 years in banking and advertising, Rudo facilitates staff training mainly in Business Etiquette/ Grooming, Service Quality, Customer Care, Communications and Time Management. Rudo is often referred to as the lemonade lady following her highly successful speeches that encourage people to put a spin to negative experiences for their good.

www.junieyeballseries.co.za

🄢 rudo.bingepingedzenga

✉ rudodzenga@gmail.com

𝒇 facebook.com/rudobingepinge-dzenga

CHAPTER 22

I ALWAYS MAKE SOME LEMONADE
By Rudo Bingepinge-Dzenga

I have no memory of my father. All I know is what I see in old photographs and from stories I've heard over the years. A lot has been said about his great looks, his unusual ability to speak well and his sense of style that was beyond his generation. I was two years old, with older brothers and sisters, when he died. My baby sister was ten days old. Right there in the middle of celebrating and welcoming a new baby is when my father was called.

Although my father was not rich there was a scramble for his material stuff after his death, even though he had left behind a widow with six children all below the age of twelve. My mother was bold enough to reject the tradition of marrying a husband's brother after death. So there we were, the six of us, starting life with nothing and depending on Mama's state registered nurse income.

My father's death heralded the start of a long journey of self-discovery that required a tremendous amount of faith. Of course hard work, hope, pain and triumph were part of the mix. Despite a future that looked bleak, Mama believed everything was going to work together for good; lemonade still had to be made from the lemons thrown at us.

Over and above his fashion sense and his oratorical skills, my father must have stood out from many other angles. His wish was to see his kids go to school and break new ground for his name and the extended family. Most of the girls in his family and the area he grew up never seemed to go beyond grade seven. They would drop out of school to have babies or get married with no sound education.

After my father died, we lived in a small township where we rented two rooms. I remember vividly how Mama, my young sister and I shared a bed, and as we grew older we moved to the floor. School was not very far but it felt far in winter when I had to walk to school in slippers. It was hard to be passionate about school for starters; I did not have the school uniform like the other kids. When I had some kind of uniform it was a hand me down that would be too small, too big or too torn and sewn far too many times. I stood out for all the wrong reasons.

The rule of attraction (some version of it!) applied even way back then. When you are scruffy and untidy it is hard to make friends at school, but I have been blessed with great solid friends who are still in my life. I am forever thankful to God for my childhood friends. They saw me with no shoes and an over-sewn uniform and liked me as I was; 35 years later I now have more pairs of shoes but they still treat me the same!

I was an entrepreneur early (we had to) to supplement Mama's income. My sisters, brothers and I sold fruits in the township. We looked forward to new houses being built; builders were good spenders, and we sold tea and sandwiches to them. Mama made use of any free land around the township which was not in use. We would grow maize, ground nuts and peanuts and weed the small fields after school. It was not cool at all even during those days but there was no time to be a full time child or time to be a cool kid.

Mama gave me the greatest gift of all; I got the freedom to dream. I dreamed big, and Mama encouraged it. She allowed us to dream. I saw myself as a university graduate, a writer, an actress on television with my own car and house. I do not know how Mama did it; it really must be hard to encourage kids to dream when the stomach is empty, but she did it. I started to believe that the lack around me was just temporary, that education was my key out.

My primary school teacher, Mrs. M, seemed especially made just for me. She enjoyed my weekly creative stories and how I delivered my poems in class. I soon realized that, despite my bare feet, I had special skills and gifts that came naturally to me. My teacher encouraged me to produce plays for Parents' Day meetings. My very first play was in commemoration of World Health Day. The play was popular at the school, which gave me confidence. I entered local speaking and acting competitions and won some cash that made a difference back home. My uniforms and slippers (or lack thereof) remained the same but I became confident that I was not poor, I was rich in something. I was determined to play to my strengths. My first paid writing article was published in a Christian magazine called Step – I was fourteen at that time.

There was little to go around. I had bare necessities and I lacked in many ways, but I had a very happy childhood. My brothers, sisters and I grew up surrounded with so much love. Mama's four brothers were fantastic father figures and "moms" too. God moved things around and planted people in our lives to satisfy certain needs. A local pastor wrote a letter to a family in the USA about a widow with six young kids. This led to a lifelong relationship with an American couple from Pennsylvania. The couple started sending us money to help with school fees. The couple also sent clothes, all the way from America from when I was about four until I went to university. The couple also paid for my very first trip to America. When I look back, I realize there were a lot more people who came in to our lives to help with specific needs.

The only university in the country at that time did not offer the programs I wanted to study. I wanted to study drama, film or music; I studied Sociology, becoming the first girl on my father's side of the family to go to University! It gives me some peace that in a way I managed to break new grounds for my father's family. I was happy to be different like my father had desired.

I kept dreaming. In the university town I auditioned for a television drama series and got one of the leading roles. Since then, I have done some short film projects as an actress and also as a script writer. God has given me a chance to do a good number of radio voiceovers too. I am not sure if my mother has anything to do with it, but I love to write about issues that affect women and children. I have since written two books. I am finalizing my first children's book, a crime buster series.

144

I do not have the formula to life, but for me it is clear that dreaming regardless of current circumstances did it. The mental decision to make lemonade with what is given to you tops it all.

My mother had literally one answer to all the problems presented to her. "Everything works together for good. Make some lemonade." It does not matter to her how complicated or sophisticated you think your problem is, her response has been the same over the years.

For those of you not familiar with the term, "make some lemonade," when someone says that to you, they are indeed acknowledging the fact that you have been through some rough times and that life has not been kind to you. But they are also challenging you not to sit and mourn forever. They are challenging you to rise and do something about your misfortune. It is about putting a spin to mess! It is about breathing life into a situation that was meant to destroy you emotionally, physically or spiritually.

When you start applying yourselves fully you will realize your strengths and make challenging experiences work in your favor. Today is the day you make some lemonade.

Lemonade making recipe:

1. Clearly identify the lemons that have been thrown at you. The good news is, when making lemonade, often you do not need to drop a dime.

2. Have a willing heart and a mind that is willing to change and learn.

3. Get rid of the foolish pride, humbling yourself for once.

4. Let go of those past hurts even when those who hurt you have not asked for forgiveness.

5. Get rid of your selfish side and experience what it is like to put others before you for a change.

6. Add some patience and determination to turn it around.

7. Mix the above with patience, dreaming big, hard work and most of all add PRAYER.

8. Now watch how everything starts to work together for good.

Warning: You may not get results right away but His timing is perfect for us. When afraid or in doubt, apply number 7 more often.

Having lemons apparently is not enough to make lemonade! Look at the back of the Lemonade bottle. There is a pinch of this, a dash of that, 0.002 grams of that, all these add up. The challenge is for us to start doing the small things, the obvious stuff that is within our control and let us see where it gets us. The truth is when we really apply ourselves fully we can always, always make some lemonade. Make some lemonade today!

Anita Sechesky

Anita is a Registered Nurse, Certified Life Coach, International Best Selling Author, Speaker, Trainer, NLP and LOA Wealth Practitioner, as well as Big Vision Consultant. She studied Marketing at the School of Online Business and completed her Advanced Certificate of Life Coaching at Academy of Coaching Cognition. She is the CEO and Owner of Anita Sechesky – Living Without Limitations. Anita has assisted many people breaking through their own limiting beliefs in life and business. She has two International Best Sellers and is compiling her third anthology "Living Without Limitations – 30 Stories to Love Your World," to be released in 2014.

You can contact Anita at the following:

www.anitasechesky.com

🅢 anita.sechesky

✉ asechesky@hotmail.ca

🅕 facebook.com/AnitaSechesky

🅕 facebook.com/asechesky

🅞 @nursie4u

🅟 pinterest.com/anitasechesky

🅛 ca.linkedin.com/pub/anita-sechesky/3b/111/8b9

CHAPTER 23

I WILL NEVER FORGET HER LAST WORDS TO ME

By Anita Sechesky

For as long as I can remember, I always had a unique perspective on life. There were even times that I felt as though no one liked or appreciated me. Many times over growing up, I recall my mom telling me not to think like that. My dear sweet mom has always been my voice of reason. When I got offended or hurt by the remarks or attitudes of others, she always told me to forgive them. Thank you, Mom but I still had to figure them out.

I could never figure out why people behaved the way they did, which is probably why I became a Registered Nurse and now a Life Coach. I love to analyze and understand others. One of my most disturbing discoveries was realizing how so many people who were mean or negative towards me were actually jealous. This was confirmed to me by a distant relative who is a well-known minister and counselor to many in New York City. He confided in me that based on what he knew already, and what God had revealed to him, that there were many individuals very close to me who were indeed jealous and I should be wary of their motives. What a confirmation and eye-opener at the same time.

So many things in my life started to make sense. I now understood the snide remarks, such as "Not everyone could be a nurse," or "I don't care if you are a nurse." How could people so close to me be so cruel and heartless? How would they feel if someone said that to their own loved one? Little did they realize how much hatred, mental and verbal abuse I had already endured during my first year of training in Nursing School. The instructors, whom I once had such high regard for, were initially pleasant and supportive of me as an eager student;

then they let me down. They did a complete switch in their response towards me during my second year of training. For unknown reasons, they changed their attitudes and behaviors towards me, even after I had successfully completed the whole first year with a perfect GPA of 4.0. What an accomplishment, considering the curriculum was part of a very prestigious university.

Although I was the only non-white student in my class, I have always chosen to look past these visible differences. My grades could not be disputed, considering the time and effort I put into my education. Based on the events that occurred at that time in my life, I can tell you that I would have never imagined in a million years people who call themselves caring professionals could be as cruel and heartless as these women were towards me. The biggest lesson I learned was that the human mind, will, and emotions play an intricate role in helping the human spirit to persevere when all hope is stolen and damaged. I am so thankful that I never committed suicide when I was in the pit of despair, feeling worn out, and struggling to survive. It was at that moment I cried out to God, asking HIM that if HE really wanted me to be a nurse, it had to be for more than just me. There must be a bigger plan and if HE wanted me to survive this living nightmare, HE would make a way when there seemed to be no way. God has proven to me that HE doesn't make junk.

Another one of the most trying and challenging times of my life was when I received a phone call in the middle of the night that my late grandmother had been taken to the Emergency Department and wasn't doing well. I recall watching Grandma as she declined in health after being admitted onto the hospital ward where I worked. It was my home floor where I started my first full-time position as an RN. I was hired as a Cardiology Nurse. Through those years, I developed some wonderful friendships, and one of my colleagues had become the Nurse Manager on the floor. When Grandma was admitted to the hospital, she had suffered multiple injuries, leaving her broken and blind in one eye. As you can imagine, it was horrific to see her in this condition. I picked up as many shifts as I could, even though I had just found out that I was pregnant with my second child. Because of the unexpected stress and emotional abuse I endured during Grandma's hospitalization from people very close to me, I was at risk of my pregnancy being terminated. My doctor scheduled weekly ultrasounds to keep track of my baby's growth and development. Grandma never fully recovered from her injuries.

But I will never forget the last words she ever said to me from her hospital bed. I had just completed my shift and this was when I could spend time alone with her without any interruptions. This particular night I was crying as I sat next to her. She said to me, "Babe, why are you crying?" I told her, "They don't like me." Grandma then said, "They don't like me either. But Jesus loves me and HE loves you and I love you too." These words are so powerful. They have more meaning than a thousand words can say.

My dear sweet deceased Grandma lived a life that is a tribute to what one person can accomplish on her own. She was a widow at 28 years of age with eight children to raise on her own. She has inspired me to realize that we don't need the praise and worship of others. We must first believe in ourselves. Grandma loved and respected everyone for who they were. She accepted each person she met in her life, never judging others, but always believing that everyone, including her grandchildren and great grandchildren, deserved to be all that they were created to be. She was proud of each and every one of them and always tried to maintain peace and unity among her family.

Her greatest desire was that all her children would come to understand the relationship she had with her Heavenly Father. Grandma's faith had brought her through some of the worst things she experienced in her lifetime. I am sure there were many that even my dad and his siblings did not know about. After all, life could not have been easy being a single mother in the 1940s and 1950s with no formal education and support of family. Yet my grandma managed to raise and educate and professionally train all of her children so they could support their own families one day. What a woman! I am so proud of the legacy she has left behind and to have known and loved her.

When my son was born I named him in honor of his late great-grandma. One day when he is older, I will tell him of the amazing woman she was, and her dream and vision for her loved ones. We can all do our part. It starts within our hearts to show others what we are made of and where we originate from.

I guess this is why I am who I am with a determined grandma who never gave up on her goals in life. It must be part of my DNA. Thank you, Dad. A mother's love continues to carry through the generations. My parents have instilled in me that it is not my problem what others think of me. Instead it becomes my problem if I choose to think less of myself.

I want to encourage you to never give up, whether on a dream, ambition, or lifelong goal. You deserve the right to have the opportunity to prove to yourself that you are more than capable. Don't listen to the lies of others. God created you perfect in HIS image. You were born for greatness. Step into the life that is waiting for you.

Maybe you have lost someone dear to you and you felt like you had no control over the circumstances to even be part of their life. I know I could have helped to make Grandma more comfortable by caring for her and giving her my love. But, the choice was not given to me even though I represented my dad as his eldest child. I always try to help others have a good life. Every human being deserves to leave this world in dignity, comfort, and pain-free. As nurses we see many things. But the hardest is to be completely helpless when it's your own loved ones.

If you are still struggling with a loss, allow yourself time to grieve and forgive what needs to be forgiven. We cannot change the past; we can only learn from it. In this life, one thing is sure; we will all come to the end of our journeys one day. What you allow for others should be exactly what you would allow for yourselves.

Valentina Gjorgievska

Valentina started her career in Community Services as a life coach/ employment coach in 2007. She has assisted many people in overcoming their limitations during this time, as well as assisting them to re-enter the workforce. Her expertise is suicide, severe mental health issues and grief or trauma. She currently works with people with disabilities and severe mental health issues nationwide across Australia. Valentina is currently completing a Psychology Degree that she put on hold after the sudden death of her father; she also has a First Aid in Mental Health. She has a passion for music and sang professionally in her younger years.

- valentinagjorgjievska
- valgjorgjievska1985@gmail.com
- facebook.com/valentina23
- facebook.com/valentina.gjorgjievska.92
- @valentinagj23
- linkedin.com/pub/valentina-gjorgjievska/87/4b7/2b7

CHAPTER 24

I NEVER GOT A CHANCE TO SAY GOODBYE

By Valentina Gjorgievska

I had the unfortunate experience at the age of 25 years old of going through a traumatic event by losing my father to a sudden and unexpected heart attack, and my world was suddenly turned upside down. I recall it being 3 years to the day in March 2014; it was a dark and stormy Saturday night in my home town of Sydney, Australia. I was just finishing my studies for Semester 1 for my first psychology assignment for the year, and I remember getting ready go out for the night but having this horrible feeling that I shouldn't be going anywhere. The feeling was intense, but I pushed it aside thinking that I was just being silly; only at that very moment my younger sister walked through my bedroom door and voiced the same concerns. We both felt it but didn't know what it was. She tried to convince me not to go out, but my friend whom I had made plans with would not take no for an answer. I tried desperately to cancel my plans to no avail.

Leaving my bedroom to go to the kitchen where the rest of the family was, I noticed that nothing seemed amiss. Mum was washing the dishes, and my brother was standing at the bench talking to her. Dad was sitting at the dining table playing with his music mixer, his headphones on, to get music ready for his upcoming tour at the end of the year, which was a daily thing for him. Nothing was out of place. Deciding against my inner intuition, I advised everyone in the room that I was leaving. As I turned to leave the kitchen something made me look at my father. He had no idea what was being said, as he did not remove his headphones off his ears, but he made eye contact with me indicating he knew I was going out. Not saying goodbye, I walked out the front door and into my friend's car against my better judgment.

Standing in the middle of a crowed night club, I looked at my phone which said it was almost 12 a.m. A few moments later I received a text message from my sister to come back home, that Dad had stopped breathing. Shock and panic overtook me as we sped in the car back home only to be too late; he was already on his way to the hospital, and it didn't look good. By exactly 12 a.m. that night, he was pronounced dead.

I never got a chance to say goodbye.

Over the course of the 2 ½ years since his death, I had changed in character and gone off track of who I was, but I was trying to find my way back. Finding that being around other people made me feel better than sitting at home, I surrounded myself with company from anyone who wanted to be around me at this very hard time without realizing they weren't the right people to be around. I had blocked out the memory of that fateful night and the events following, although I remembered everything about my father during his life. If my friends started talking about death, I would either leave the room or would distract myself to not listen to the conversation. It was too traumatic for me.

I experienced sharp pains in my chest, similar to a heart attack sensation for almost 12 months. My friends noticed that I started to withdraw and I was no longer interested in the things that we used to do or talk about. I developed a weaker version of my character for the course of two years that people took advantage of. I did not have the energy to defend myself, and I became overly sensitive. Being known as the brains of the family, it was a shock to everyone that I could no longer think straight. I didn't realize it, but there was a change in the dynamics of my relationship with my mother. She was going through her own grieving process, but I became very overprotective of her constantly, like I was the parent. I wouldn't let her out of my sight, because I feared of losing her the same way.

My connection and bond with my father was a very close and strong one, being that we were a very close and happy family. I grew up in a happy home and had the best of everything, which made his death even harder, especially knowing what his plans were for the future. As time goes on, memories will also trigger these emotions. Being that he was a musician, quiet was not a normal day in our household. We were taught that life is music. An average day for us at home was 5 different types of live music blaring from 5 different corners of the house all at the same time. Quiet did not exist in our household. But when he passed away, due to religious beliefs, the house was quiet.

Just weeks before he passed away he sat me down as if knowing what was going to happen, and he told me what he wanted me to do and to listen to him and no one else. This kept repeating itself in my mind and kept me going throughout the whole ordeal. My strength of character also assisted me to keep going – I was the strongest in the family. I overcame not only my own grief and despair but also carried my mother, brother and sister to overcome their own.

The recovery process has taken almost three years and is still continuing as there is no time limit to grief. I was very close to my Dad and surviving his death was not an easy journey. The connection between me and my Dad has not been broken in spirit, and I will always be daddy's little girl.

"You'll always be in my heart.
In loving memory
To my Dad"
Love,
Tina

In my career, I had assisted many clients in overcoming trauma and grief. But it wasn't until I went through it myself that I actually fully understood what they went through. I found that a lot of people don't understand what it is like to lose someone close to you, and how the mind reacts and copes. I found myself saying to a lot of people that they didn't understand, a statement that I hear also from a lot of my clients.

So how did I survive this very traumatic event in my life?

- My strength of character
- My bond with my immediate family – my mother, brother and sister
- Holding on to Dad's last words to me and my memories of him
- I appreciated what he valued in his life that made him unique, such as his music
- His quirky sense of humor and his strange musical habits
- The values that he taught me and the things that he encouraged me to do

If you have lost someone close to you, you may want to write a memory list to help you overcome your loss.

Grieving is not a mental illness, even though you may show signs of post-traumatic stress disorder. Each person goes through their own experience of grief and loss; it is not the same across the board, it's an individual experience. You may experience several of the following: physical distress such as chest pains, change in appetite, weight change, crying, feelings of emptiness, extreme anger, irritability, guilt, loneliness, vulnerability, feelings of abandonment, being overly sensitive, dependence on others, being withdrawn, avoiding other people, lack of interest in things and people, forgetfulness, searching for the deceased, not thinking clearly, trying not to talk about death and needing to retell the story.

Here are some things to remember and incorporate in your daily routine while going through these stages. Do not compare your experience to someone else's – everyone mourns and reacts differently. Talk to others that you can trust, but be careful whom you trust – there are many people out there who have not experienced losing someone and do not understand what you are going through, possibly deterring you in your recovery process. Introduce pleasant changes in your life; make plans to assist you to survive the weekends. It may be difficult to be motivated to go out, but it is very important in order for your mind to stay clear that you do not confine yourself to home. Understand that any feelings that you are going through are the normal grief reaction; until you are out of the grieving stages do not make any major life decisions. Do not listen to other people if they pressure you in any way – listen to yourself; you best know how you feel. Do things that you enjoy and that bring you happiness; be around positive people, do not sit alone during this time.

Gloria Delvecchio Callan

Born in Montreal, with a rich Italian background, Gloria studied in a French milieu which gives her a knowledge of many languages, as well as flair and joy in living a vibrant life. Her educational background with an RN degree and a marketing degree in the fashion industry makes her very flexible to an individual's needs. Gloria practiced as an RN for over 20 years in many fields, including pediatrics, surgery, orthopedics and infertility. Her research and extensive travels in Europe and South America led her to a degree as a Health Educator and Diet Counselor. Gloria faced and survived cancer herself without conventional medicine. She now teaches clients to take control of their health. She empowers and teaches through the process of nutrition and lifestyle changes to reverse the effects of many acute and chronic diseases. She addresses the immediate symptoms as well as examining the underlying causes of health issues. Gloria's clients state that "You are promised a passionate and supportive partnership for your long-term health." She does private consultations with personalized programs as well teaching for small or large companies who want better health for their workers.

It's time for you and the next generation to take the "dis" out of disease and live your life with ease. Fix it with food.

Contact Gloria today for your session to a better and healthy you.

 bglo@rogers.com

CHAPTER 25

THE CROSSROAD TO MY HEALING

By Gloria Delvecchio Callan

You have all heard the following expression many times before; live your life with "childlike faith." I remember feeling as a child that nothing was impossible and dreaming I could accomplish anything I set my mind to do. I believed, and I saw everyone through rose-colored lenses.

In my childhood I had parents who were very different. My dad was a very handsome man who smiled all the time and loved everyone he met. He constantly told me that he loved me and encouraged me to chase all my dreams, and that nothing was impossible to learn and achieve. Yet he had a personal problem with drinking. On the other hand my mom was a disciplinarian; she never told me she loved me but had high expectations and demanded perfection. That was ok, because I loved my parents so much and wanted to please them. Therefore, I excelled at everything – academics, sports and relationships. My reasoning was that I wanted them to be proud of me.

When I was in high school, my parents were constantly fighting, and I was desperate to get away from the fighting at home. I traveled by bus every day for four years and to attend a small church chapel inside a hospital across the street from my high school. I believed there was something peaceful inside this place. This was a pivotal time in my life that would later prove to be a life preserver.

After high school I wanted to follow my heart and decided on a nursing career to help people who were in need. Unfortunately, I finished school at an early age and this dream was put on hold. As my parents grew further apart, I had no direction or mentors to guide me in life. I met a man that was nine years older than me, whom I believed was going to give me a chance to have all I ever needed – children, a stable home and a way to fill the void in my heart. We faced many bumps in the road and surprises as we attempted to achieve a successful marriage and a stable life together.

Now, let us fast forward to four years later. We had two children, a girl and a boy whom I dearly loved. All was going according to plan, and my dream of having my own family was realized. Not so fast. My dad passed away from cancer; he was only 52. I was devastated and overwhelmed with grief. I never processed my grief for him, and my life felt like a car that was stuck in a ditch spinning and getting nowhere.

Now the ruts in the ditch got worse and I found myself pregnant with a third child in the winter after my dad passed away. My husband did not want another child and I was filled with tremendous anxiety at the prospect of having another child. At the time I was only 21 and my children were ages two and one. My husband was starting down a path of excessive drinking. To make matters worse, he told me, "I really did not want any children." The decision which I made changed the course of my life forever. Yes! I made the decision to abort this pregnancy. This did not come easily; I was scared, with no one to talk to, since abortion was not an issue talked about in the seventies. I would look at my children, the joy they brought to my life every day and would ask myself, "How can you think of an abortion?" Tears would just roll down my face like floodwaters.

As the days drifted by, I was taking care of my children with no participation from my husband. My mother was always criticizing me about how I raised my children. I was sinking like quicksand, and I had no one to turn to. I made all the arrangements for the abortion. I found a baby sitter for the children and traveled to the United States by myself in the middle of winter to have this miserable procedure done in a small dingy clinic. The doctor explained that they would use a suction procedure and it would be all be over in thirty minutes, and I would be able to go home in two hours.

The nurses were cold as they were doing their duties, as if it were a menial task like washing dishes – no compassion, no caring. The moments after the procedure left a hole in my heart like a tornado ripping it into million pieces, because I overheard the nurses say that the child was a boy!

I came home bleeding from the procedure; I was numb and felt ice cold like I had died but was still alive. It was surreal. I cared for my two children over the next days, months and years with love and cherished every moment with them. Yet my heart ached always for the child I lost, and I would become depressed or get very ill every year at the time my son would have been born. I was so bruised from this event that led to many crossroads in my life. It made me bitter, angry, depressed, jealous, selfish, unforgiving towards others, and determined that I was going to live a life of "doing it my way." I had lost my childlike faith and became very critical and judgmental. This contributed to feelings of unworthiness, an attempted suicide, and finally a divorce and a life as a single mom, with all its challenges. I just wanted to scream at the doctor who did the procedure and let him know that it was not over in thirty minutes. This nightmare affected me for a lifetime.

Four years later, hope was on the horizon. God's plan for me led me to my present husband of thirty years. With him, I have survived many crossroads filled with rebellious children, sickness, death of loved ones, and loss of jobs – yet he loved me unconditionally. He could not understand my deep-seeded feelings of shame and guilt from a mistake I had made in the past. I had kept this secret for over thirty years. I was parched and thirsty for relief, looking for a well in this desert of pain.

Then out of desperation I turned to Jesus for help and hope, but my hurt was so deep that it took another seven years, going through many disappointments, and most importantly not being able to let go of past mistakes. Life has way of presenting you with a horrible tragedy that is wrapped up in a beautiful gift box waiting for you to peel off the paper and find inner strength. I was diagnosed with breast cancer. Yes, the ultimate crossroad. My life came to a screeching halt.

Now I turn my attention to the women and men reading this story. The above is an event in my life that might have happened to you also. As you can now see, the last crossroad for me was when I came to the end of myself and had no choice but surrender. This was when I met my Savior face to face and heard his sweet voice whisper in my ears of how much He loved me and that "I WAS WHOLE AND HEALED BY HIS STRIPES." This happened at Mount Sinai Hospital on December 13, 2010, just when I had been told that I had a 16% chance to live.

I was overwhelmed, but at the same time filled with instant peace. His peace.

For some of you right now you are skeptical and do not believe in miracles. That is ok, because He loves you so much and has so much grace as well as mercy that He will allow you to make the decision to reveal Himself to you. I spent the next six months developing my relationship with Him and was freed of all bitterness, anger, and forgave all who hurt me. I had no more jealousy and apologized to my husband and my children for the hurts that I may have caused in their lives. My broken and shattered heart was touched by a father's love from above, and in return gave me a life free of shame and guilt for the horrible mistake I made in having an abortion.

This is when my crossroad to true healing happened. I was now truly a whole person and could live my life with true joy and peace.

I meditated on many verses to help me overcome my feeling of guilt and shame. Trust me, you need to know that you too are worthy of total forgiveness and find inner healing by forgiving yourselves as well.

He created you in your mother's womb, He has great plans for you, and nothing you do is a surprise to Him. If you look up the word laminin, it is the glue that holds your cells together in your DNA. Inside there is a shape of a cross – His imprint is in your DNA.

He knows the number of hairs you have on your head. Don't be afraid; He takes care of the birds and the flowers in the fields, therefore to Him you are definitely more valued and loved than them. He knows every aspect of your body, mind, soul as well as all your needs. Can you imagine that!

The Lord has great plans for you. He wants to aid you and not harm you; He wants to give you hope and a future. He will guide you through your challenges, disappointments, failures, and hardships of life, because His promises are true and you can count on them. God loved you so much that gave his one and only Son, Jesus, to die for you. The power of his death on the cross is all about this statement, "It is finished." That statement was just for you, He has forgiven you of every mistake and wrong you have done in the past, present and in the future. You are now in right-standing with God. No more guilt, shame, bitterness, anger, revenge or jealousy. You will be filled with His love because He took all your hurts to the Cross. He has forgiven you! For the men reading this, I plead with you to get involved, be supportive and please do not judge her decision. Remember it is your love and compassion that will heal her heart.

You too will also have joy once again and will live a vibrant life that looks like a rainbow after a thunderstorm. Today I have total health. I now have a degree in nursing, and practice as a health educator and diet counselor. I teach people the benefits of disease prevention, which includes inner healing as well as outer healing and impacting people's lives every day. I have childlike faith despite the event in my life that could have stolen every joy that God had planned for me.

I now live my life with gratitude every day, because of the blessings He has given me in life. There are too many for me to mention, but I will share just this one. I now have a new son, I call him my adoptive son, and his name is Charlie. He came into my life with his wife Adrianna at the same time that I discovered I had cancer. He was there for every step climbing the mountain in my fight against cancer.

The miracle is in God's timing because the child that I aborted would have been born at the same time that Charlie was born. Yes, God does heal all wounds and meets you at every crossroad in your life. Just receive it and believe it. God is in the details. God is in the moment. God is in all parts of your life, even the hurts in life.

Life is like a dessert. Too brief to hurry. On the other hand too short not to let Him in your life.

What is healing? We all have a different perspective of this powerful word. As for me, it is knowing that Christ lives in me and nothing is impossible because He loves me. I will leave you with a parting message that children are like angels from heaven and working with them as a nurse gave me back my childlike faith once more. Because when you look in their eyes, that is what you see. They want to get better and they just believe. You too can be healed. Just believe!

This is a special message to women contemplating an abortion; there is a heartbeat at day twenty-one, brainwaves on day forty-five! That's right, even before you know there is a pregnancy. This is a special gift from God and He will bring you through this with His love and promises.

You too can be a whole person and have your crossroad to healing.

Let your heart be healed. Just let Him in, He will be the greatest connection and relationship you will ever have for living your life without limitations.

Janel Simpson

Janel Simpson is a Youth Counselor, Spiritual Life Coach, Trainer, and Speaker. She is the CEO and Founder of Emmanuel Life Management Center. She holds a Bachelor's Degree in Sociology and Criminology. Janel is a Visionary whose purpose is to transform lives.

Over the last 10 years Janel has mentored youth and families going through rough times.

Janel's vision for her charity is to see Canadian youth truly liberated socially, academically, and spiritually to take on their God-given purpose to serve their families and communities.

She is an extraordinary mother and role model to her son. Janel is passionate about life.

You can contact Janel at:

www.emmanuellifemanagementcenter.com

✉ **simpsonjanel@hotmail.com**

✉ **elmc2010@hotmail.ca**

f **facebook.com/emmanuel10101010**

f **facebook.com/janel.simpson.71**

🐦 **twitter.com/elmc2010**

CHAPTER 26

DEATH CALLED ME BUT MY DESTINY ANSWERED!

By Janel Simpson

Looking back it seems like yesterday. I can still remember the loud BANG, which turned out to be gunshots firing. I remembered my friend standing next to me yelling at me to run; before I knew it I got hit. I remember every emotion that came from being in that position. I was in a state of shock while lying on the ground, in and out of consciousness waiting for the ambulance. My Dad calling my name every five seconds, telling me to hold on. I was tired and felt numb, and yet I was afraid and lonely. I started feeling a strange separation that I could not understand. Everything was happening just so FAST. It felt as if I was trying to keep up with time, but time was not waiting for me. In the ambulance I heard the emergency vehicles around me. I felt rushed trying to make it to the hospital before it was too late.

It was a beautiful summer evening and my family and friends were planning a back to school BBQ. I was excited and anxious to see all my loved ones united together. I recalled that night I was doing up those hamburgers and BBQ chicken on the grill. Great music, food and weather; this was truly fun times. By the time I realized, it was almost midnight.

My favorite part of the night was hugging and kissing everyone goodbye. The last thing I remember was laughing with my good friends in the front yard. As we exchanged kind words and well wishes I heard a loud BANG coming from the fences by the road. Little did I know, this was the beginning of a top story in the newspaper. Surprisingly, I got shot and fell to the ground unable to move. As I lay on the ground wounded and helpless, the only question I asked myself was, "Who could have done this?" Furthermore, I could not put a face to any person I know that would want me dead. I began questioning myself to find out if I might have hurt someone unknowingly. Nothing was making sense at this point, because there was no justifiable explanation. The police investigators labeled the case, "Mistaken Identity." They themselves were unable to find any suitable evidence for an attempted murder case.

The Hospital was my worst nightmare, as I tasted and felt the call of death. As my body was undergoing surgery, the only thing that was going through my mind was, I have to complete University. In the days and weeks that followed, I was afraid of losing a limb or some part of my body. I remembered telling my mind that I have not lived my life as yet; I am too young to die. I began looking at my future ahead with the spirit of a fighter. I have never desired to live as much as I did at that point. It was as if I was willing to offer anything just to have a second chance at life. It sounds strange, but I was better able to see my future looking through the eyes of my pain. I realized that the answers lie within me, and I can choose to live or die.

At this point I was consumed with my own thoughts of how to survive. My physical body and mind were telling my spiritual man to work in unity and give me the will to survive. As a teenager I could not help but wonder how my life would change after surgery. I asked myself, "Will I be able to walk again? Will my friends like me the same? Will this horrible and debilitating pain endure forever? Will I ever walk around my neighborhood feeling safe?" I often wondered if these shooters would ever come after me again. It was painful wondering what a normal life would be like.

As a University student my whole world was shaken. I lost my passion and drive for many things, including sports and leisure activities. I could not concentrate on my studies because of the tragic playback in my mind. For many years I despised any loud BANG, abrupt sound or flashing lights. I went through psychological counseling at the university, where I was able to open up the pain and hurt that I was feeling.

Over time, this tragedy caused me to become more mature and responsible. In fact I began looking at life differently. As a teenager growing up with a Christian background, it was important to have Faith. The pain became the least of my worries when I started believing by faith for the best. I began having visions and dreams about my future. My passions for life were now becoming alive again. I found myself in a place of peace and seclusion. My eyes were now opened to understand the power of destiny within me. It was at this point that destiny gave birth in my mind, and life began.

During my recovery I discovered that life has a purpose for me. Once I acknowledged that purpose, anything that comes to rob me of life should be a fight until the end. It doesn't matter what my circumstances are, whether it be sickness or death. My role is to make sure I make the best decisions concerning my life. Unfortunately for me, I identified my purpose when I was on the hospital bed. I learned sometimes we have to be in an uncompromising position to identify our self-worth. I did not answer to the call of death because I knew there was greatness in store for my future.

My biggest breakthrough came when I learned to forgive and let go fear. It released me from the pain, anger, frustration and hurt. Forgiveness was a major healing device for me to recover and maintain a sound mind. It released my mind from fear and rebuilt my faith to trust again. I was tired of feeling a sense of bitterness or expecting some sort of equal compensation. I discovered there is no such thing when trying to overcome any situation. I was able to identify the damage and forgive to start the healing process within my mind. The overall healing was only possible when I came to understand and experience the power of holding on to my faith. Through it all, I never doubted God and his Will to deliver me from all my fears. I would say my best experience with God was at my weakest point. Amazingly, God has a way of revealing his love and strength in these times to prove he is Almighty God.

KEYS TO YOUR DESTINY

I want to inspire you to overcome failures and pursue your "purpose" to fulfill your destiny. Your purpose is that which you are passionate about and hold dear to your heart. Finding your passion is never easy; but when you come to that place in your life, living is more fulfilling.

Now I understand why the adversary would want to take you out of this life before your God-given purpose is fulfilled. It is that purpose that reveals your destiny and fulfills your life. If you accept the defeat of sickness or death in your mind, you are taking the risk of killing your purpose and terminating your destination. Sadly, life is not promised to anyone. However, the worst is to know that you can innocently step outside and lose your life because of someone else's ignorance. The "fear factor" usually comes when you understand how one person could have control over another.

Do not allow this healing process to be hindered by a lack of forgiveness, fear to trust, fear of the unknown, fear of turning your back on someone, or even the fear of evil that resides in people. The more you seek God for answers to questions about life, the more you will gain wisdom. When you realize how to apply wisdom to life's situations, fear is expelled from your existence. Your passion and purpose is in your heart, and it has no fear. In fact, God has orchestrated your life to be lived in boldness and fearlessness.

Having a Mind to survive is your primary key to destiny. Death does not have any control over your future. Do not give up on life, because life will not give up on you. No man knows his destiny until he finds God in his heart. There are no boundaries or limitation to this great vision and dream God has for you. Understanding who you are, why you were born, and where you are going is half way to destiny. Live your life with genuine passion because your destiny is unstoppable.

We all have a destiny, a journey to be completed, and one that is already written. It is my hope to see you all discover your purpose, dream big, follow your vision and pursue success and happiness.

Kristy-Lea Tritz

Kristy-Lea Tritz is an International Bestselling Author. She also coaches women in her program "A Woman's Voice!" and is the host of her own radio show. Her freelance work has appeared in Brio magazine and local publications. Currently she is working on her first children's book and first anthology in the "A Woman's Voice!" series. Kristy-Lea also has a passion for special needs children and is currently working on developing products for children and their parents who are affected by A.D.H.D. When she is not exercising her creative side, she is most likely spending active time with her husband Sebastien and son Jacob. You can connect with Kristy-Lea at

www.kristyleatritz.com

✉ **contact@kristyleatritz.com**

f **facebook.com/kristyleatritzwrites#**

🐦 **twitter.com/kristyleatritz**

▶ **youtube.com/kristyleatritz**

g+ **google.com/+KristyLeaTritzwrites**

in **ca.linkedin.com/in/kristyleatritz**

CHAPTER 27

INNOCENCE LOST: A CHILD'S CRY IN THE DARK!

By Kristy-Lea Tritz

"Whoa!" Dad leapt up from his seated position on the couch. Looking each one of us four girls in the eyes, he said, "Looks like we have to choose better next time. Sorry, girls, this one we can't watch." He took the video from the VCR.

Sex scenes in movies were not something I was exposed to as a child. If it was a small scene, like a kissing scene, it was fast-forwarded. Sex scenes, especially at the beginning of a movie, immediately meant it was turned off, no questions asked. As a child, I understood that it was one way by which my parents were trying to instill within us God's design for sex. A way in which to preserve our innocence as children.

To be completely honest, I don't have many memories from when I was a child. It is almost as if the time has been erased from my memory. At age seven, a sexual trauma occurred. It was a trauma that acted like a switch and turned some of my memories back on. Age four or five was the first time I had been sexually assaulted. It was something that had been repressed so deeply. Here I was a child. A small, innocent child dealing with a trauma that most adults have a hard time dealing with. How do you overcome something like this? So I did the only thing I knew how to do. I tried to forget it ever happened. I tried to erase the memory completely.

Fast forward to age sixteen. Now I was allowed to date! Inside I wasn't excited for this time of my life; I was terrified. Terrified because by this time I had already experienced sexual assault and rape several times. All the trauma I had gone through was shaping me into a person who lived in fear. I was crippled by it. I hated leaving my house. I turned within. I learned well how to hide behind a smile. Feelings of shame, guilt, disappointment and worthlessness embraced me. I felt dirty and like somehow it happened because I didn't do something. I was able to completely separate from myself. When in the throes of a traumatic experience I was able to separate from it so much that I often had no idea what happened. It frustrated me beyond words that my body would do this. I didn't want to be a victim again! I wanted to fight not freeze! Every part of me cried out in silence but no one could hear the deep wound being ripped into the very core of me. I was alone! God was the only one who heard me cry, who caught every tear I shed. I had faith and I wasn't about to let that be ripped from me to.

At the Edge Fest Concert in 1996, my knight in shining armor appeared. Although I was abandoned by "friends," he was taking me under his wing. I fell hard and fast. He was the kind of guy I always dreamed of. Thoughtful, kind, compassionate and oh so sweet. Shortly into the relationship, he told me he wanted to get married. I was hooked.

He dined me and bought me beautiful things that he had to work three jobs to get. He was truly the man of my dreams. We made a pact together that we would have no sexual contact during our courtship. I thought I was finally safe. But reality hit like a ton of bricks! A switch went off within a year and soon the man I loved changed. He began asking me to wear sexy clothes which he picked out. I began eating less because he wanted me to look more like my skinnier sister. Insecurities crept in, and all the trauma I had been in took over.

Every form of abuse happened in that relationship. I lived four years in a fearful hell! I hated hearing the phone ring. I withdrew and internalized. I began having panic attacks, became anorexic and slowly died from the inside out. One day my dad took me aside and asked me where the bite mark on my arm came from. I knew he knew something was terribly wrong. I cried my eyes out till no more tears would flow. Years of unshed tears flowed throughout the conversation. I spoke with our country parish priest which gave me the courage to end the relationship. I wanted desperately to be married, to be wanted, to be loved and cared for. I was an empty shell. In the wake of it all ending, I didn't know who I was as a person. I had no idea how to make my own decisions. I was vulnerable and confused.

Now twenty-one years old, I had no sense of direction and fell into a deep unending pit of loneliness. Out of that place of loneliness, feeling completely lost, I became pregnant. I had just turned twenty-two, and here I was pregnant with my little boy. My life needed to change. I could feel God calling me out of the pit of darkness. My son was going to need a healthy, strong mother, and I wanted nothing but the best for him. I reached out for help and saw an amazing counselor/coach. She mentored me and helped me to come through that dark place into the light of real life in Christ. Here was someone in my life I could have safety with. We journeyed together for three years which were filled with tears, anger and oh, so much healing. For the first time in my life I felt whole, complete, strong, and I knew that even though all the trauma I went through was painful, someday God was going to use it for good.

Out of all that has happened to me, there is one thing in my reflecting and working backwards that I wish others had seen. It is my hope that by sharing my story with others, they will see in turn if this is happening to children around them. I couldn't have sleepovers because I feared being alone; when in Brownies, I couldn't do the campouts and often experienced anxiety just going to the meetings. I used to stand at my window every morning when my dad would go to work and cry. I didn't want him to leave – he was my protection!

Listen to what your children are telling you – not with their words but with their actions. Oftentimes children will tell you something is wrong by the way they act and react to daily situations. I can't stress enough how important it is to make time as parents to truly pay attention to our children. Put down the phones! Listen to them, pay attention to what they are doing and who they are with. As a woman who has gone through this time and time again, I know that sexual assault doesn't have a specific face. It can be a peer the same age, same sex, a cousin, a relative, a stranger, anyone! Regardless of the face it wasn't your fault and you do have a voice that needs to be heard!

I knew my pain was going to become my purpose in life. I wasn't going to be a victim any longer, I was going to be victorious! Every step of the way I was learning that no matter how much trauma, no matter your situation and no matter your circumstances, if you continue to nurture your spirit you'll no longer just live, you will thrive! My journey brought me to a place not only of amazing self exploration but to a place where I was now ready and able to reach out to others in a similar situation. I wanted them to know they are not alone!

5 STARTING STEPS TO HEALING

Find support: We are not meant to carry the burdens of trauma alone! Pain thrives in the silence; don't let yourself live in its shadows! You can't change what happened to you, but you can change what the future will be like. *Please make sure you get support from professionals in your community.

Pray: Your greatest ally is prayer. Your spirit can be rocked to the core when you have lived through trauma. Immerse yourself in prayer! Feel yourself being held in the healing arms of God. Your spirit can't heal if it remains in a place of pain!

Journal: Write it down in a safe place! Get it out! Acknowledge your feelings. You can't heal what you don't acknowledge.

Nurture: Painful trauma can bring us to place where negative feelings can take over. Nurture yourself! If you can't take care of yourself, you can't care for those around you in health.

Discover: Discover what it is like to separate yourself from pain with joy! If you can't feel joy you'll begin to forget and the pain will take over. Find your passion!

Elizabeth Ann Pennington

Elizabeth Ann Pennington is a Certified Life Coach, Best Selling International Author, Speaker, Trainer and Mentor. Elizabeth co-authored "Living Without Limitations-30 Mentors to Rock Your World" with the chapter titled "Cultivating Confidence – One Seed at a Time." She is also a member of the International Coaching Federation. She received her coaching credentials from School of Coaching Cognition and serves as a coach on Coaching Cognition's platform. Elizabeth offers her clients a safe place to find balance, embracing life one step at a time building self-confidence to live life as they desire.

www.coachingcognition.com/ElizabethPennington

www.theagetolearn.com

🅢 elizabeth.ann.pennington

✉ eapennington@outlook.com

🅕 facebook.com/elizabeth.a.pennington.3

🐦 twitter.com/ElizAnnPenn

CHAPTER 28

HEALING MY SPIRIT AND BROKEN WING

By Elizabeth Ann Pennington

I FORGIVE. Those two words are the most important and precious words in life, at least in mine.

I have three sisters, five brothers, my mommy, daddy and a grandmother we all call "Mother." We live on a farm in a very small community called Lily, Kentucky. We grow our own vegetables in the summer, canning them as they are ready and enjoying them in the winter. We also raise hogs and cattle and preserve our own meat. My clothes are homemade; I'm the grandest and best dressed little girl in the neighborhood. I love the winter time, because I get two new night gowns made of "outing" material and they match my mommy's gowns. I'm blessed, most of all blessed with lots of love and attention, being the last born and very much unexpected. That's another story!

When I think back to my childhood to tell my story, I really don't know where to start; my life has been very complicated. Here is how life looked to me in childhood:

My daddy has died and it's my fault....

My brother, just older than myself, and I are in grade school; I am only seven. Another brother is in college. The rest of my brothers and sisters have married. Daddy is postmaster at Lily, and Mommy helps him in the office. The Post Office is next door to our home, so every day after school I go straight to see Daddy to give him a hug and kiss.

Today, Mother gets my brother and me ready for school; Mommy and Daddy have already gone to work. After school, I am so excited about a girlfriend coming to play with me I go home to change into play clothes instead of going to see Daddy. While I am changing clothes, my brother comes running into the house screaming "Daddy's dead." I was Daddy's girl, and my world just stopped. It could not be true. I ran to the Post Office only to be stopped from entering. I thought that he had died because I didn't give him a hug and kiss!

I still have Mommy, Mother and brother at home, but it is not the same; I'm helpless. I once saw a bird with a broken wing; that is how I feel, broken.

As time passes, Mommy makes my brother let me go with him to do chores. This means just let me go along, I think! He takes me with him but I know he doesn't like taking his little sister with him when milking the cows, feeding the pigs and chickens. I think it's fun; but my brother doesn't. I'm having so much fun, just being with my brother, "helping" him.

This brother was not the only one I seemed to bother with my tagalongs. Once when my brother that was in college came home, Mommy insisted he and his girlfriend (now his wife) take me bowling with them. I don't think the girlfriend liked my tagging along; they didn't talk the whole way home. Mommy said it was because I beat the girlfriend's score! I'm not so sure and don't know what I have done wrong this time.

No matter the occasion, whether it is at school, at church or a community activity, I had to attend. Supposedly, keeping me busy will help me get over Daddy's death and feeling lonely.

I am now a teenager, and either too young or too old. "You cannot do that you are a girl." "You're too young," or "You cannot do that; you are too old." Please! Where do I fit in?

Skipping a few years….

I want to tell someone but can't tell anyone what's happen. Someone very close to me, someone I love and look up to has betrayed me. I'm only fourteen. I'm being sexually molested. I don't know what to do. Do I dare tell? He will be mad and not love me anymore; my sister will not believe me and will stop loving me. I've tried to stop him from touching me, but he tells me I'm going to be the one in trouble – it's my fault. People will think I'm bad, no good. I must not tell anyone, just keep it a secret here in my hiding place and hope it stops. I just have to make sure there's no possible way he will be alone with me. My spirit has been stolen.

It had started with just a touch at first; one made by accident I thought. Then it happened again and again. I tried stopping him by raising my voice telling him to stop. When someone would check to see what was happening he made a joke of it saying, "Oh, we were just horsing around."

Then he started asking Mommy's permission to let me go places with him. He always asks her in a way that indicated I wanted to go. Sometimes I could talk my way out of going. Unfortunately, there were too many times I failed.

The touching escalated. He started running his hands to places they had no business going. Then, the day came that forever altered my life.

As time passes me by….

I continue to feel guilt for my daddy's death. I pray the time will come that I will understand.

It is difficult to describe my feelings of the molestation. Emotions of fear hurt and guilt would be only a start. The feeling of abandonment is like a shadow holding me hostage. Trusting is very tough.

Countless times I've wanted to speak out, only to doubt myself. Would it be the best thing to do, will it open doors of criticism and shame to my family? What will my family and friends think of me? Will friends continue to call me friend? Will family support me?

Until the right time, I must hide my tears behind a smile and my fears behind a positive attitude.

In reflection of my past I suffered quietly for many years after Daddy died. I was just a little girl who lost her father; it happens, right? My family tried to fill my life with what they thought was best for me, and I will always love them for that. However, what I needed was to understand Daddy's death. What I heard that day was Daddy's heart broke. To me, I broke it and I would have rather have died than to have broken Daddy's heart.

Years later, while talking with my brother, I spoke of my feelings. To my surprise, he told me he had blamed himself for Daddy's death. This opened my eyes; no one knows what's in someone else's mind, how they perceive life, and how a little thing like a word can change your life forever. After the conversation with my brother, my broken wing started to heal. I no longer felt alone. Someone else has felt the same as me.

Until you let go of what you are holding in, you will never heal. I encourage everyone; please speak with someone, a family member, a friend or a professional.

Fitting in is not important to anyone except oneself. The only place anyone should worry about fitting in is with themselves and what they believe in. Nothing or no one else matters as much. I can say from personal experience of trying to "fit in," one will only find heartache and hurt feelings, not to mention the loss of time and energy so critical to having a wonderful life. With help, I took inventory of my life to separate what I needed to hang onto and what to let go of.

Violation of one's person is something that takes time to heal. I will forever have the memory but I no longer will let it hurt me. I kept this secret for most of my life until one night a deep voice from inside said to me, "It's time to let go." Even though scared, I did. Time stood still with flashbacks of those horrible times rolling in fast as I spoke. However after the words, "I've been molested" left my lips, I could feel my spirit freed.

Healing starts first by forgiving oneself; I accepted I had done nothing wrong. If something similar has happened to you, chances are you have done nothing either. You are the same wonderful person; being molested doesn't mean you're evil or bad.

After forgiving yourself, forgiving the person that molested you is a crucial final step. It has taken a lot of prayers and tears to get me to this place in life. I'm no longer afraid to look in the mirror.

Sharing my secret with the world gives strength to my healing. Ultimate healing will come when someone else's spirit and broken wing begins to heal after reading this chapter of my life.

Forgive yourself and others. Christ Jesus has and will forgive us.

Stacey Cargnelutti

Stacey injects you with pure passion! She awakens the human spirit with eternal truth that heals, frees and launches souls into destiny. Her energy is contagious, and the inspired words that flow from her heart restore and redeem lives by stirring up the unfailing love of God woven into the fiber of all mankind.

Stacey lives an inspired life of health and abundance and encourages all to life, liberty and the pursuit of happiness through her work as an author, speaker, coach and creator. She has helped many to transition from the stormy seas of life to the calm landing of sandy beaches. It is at the water's edge that her work is showcased.

Contact Stacey at:

www.staceyc.com

✉ stacey@staceyc.com

f facebook.com/staceyccom

f facebook.com/stacey.cargnelutti

🐦 Stacey@Stacey43759650

in linkedin.com/profile/view?id=198977769&trk=nav_ responsive_tab_profile_pic

CHAPTER 29

I WAS LIVING ON THE EDGE

By Stacey Cargnelutti

"Mom, what's your biggest regret?" asked my twelve-year old son. "Hmmm, I don't have any regrets…just lessons learned," I cautiously responded. "Mom, what's the worst thing you ever did?" "Ugh!" I thought, "I'm not getting off the hook here am I?"

After a sobering moment I humbly replied, "The lies."

~~~~~~~~

There was something about living on "the edge" that made me feel alive… and something about hiding that made me feel safe.

On the outside I appeared quiet, but on the inside, the noise resounded continually. Soon I found ways to escape it and began to live a double life as a result.

I listened hard, to anyone, and I watched…a lot. I was sincerely intrigued with people. But in all my observations, I neglected to develop my own identity, discover my own values, and connect with my own source of inspiration.

By the age of twelve I had already put on a mask of deceit and come to some serious resolutions on how I would live life. As I continued in conversation with my own son, it seemed that he as well, was coming to some resolutions of his own, at the ripe old age of twelve.

~~~~~~~~

It was an astounding experience to look at college photos and wonder, "Who is that?" As I turned the pages, attempting to reminisce,

I couldn't find the person in the photos, she was empty, void of substance, yet full of such presence.

Although I knew the strength of my will and the longing of my heart, I couldn't seem to connect as I continued through the album. I carried a deep desire to know love, just as every human soul, but hadn't found my worth or met my Maker.

I saw fear, along with a desperate need to know and be known, but I would lose myself in a relationship, making the prospect of intimacy terrifying.

The pervasive darkness in my green eyes spoke not only of an absence of light, but sadness, shame, and heaviness. Although comfortable teaching and performing, I hid behind alcohol and other vices to mask insecurity.

I learned to carry the emotional needs of others through cautious behavior. I chose "what, how and when," according to "their vibes" rather than my own. Ultimately, I gave my power away by allowing fear-based anger to control me.

I was the queen of deceit, well able to put on a happy face while submerged in a sea of defiance and passive aggression; soon I would be washed ashore.

By the age of twenty-three my goals were met and I thought I'd let loose and enjoy life a bit. Short of having kids and becoming a published author, I thought I had "arrived." HA!

New career, marriage, condo, mortgage, dog, friends, car... Now what? Within months, my lack of vision resulted in complete lawlessness, and this "disciplined doer" suddenly cast off all restraint, and began to live her already "double life" with greater fervency than ever before. The defiant chameleon learned how to put on many fronts.

Years of lying, stealing, addiction, compulsion, eating disorders, selfish ambition, two abortions, two adulterous relationships, a totaled car, arrest for drunk driving, and a few hours in jail with a cell full of prostitutes, resulted.

My deep seated belief that "love is dangerous," continued to confirm itself as I sabotaged every attempt at true connection and intimacy. Before long, I found myself in a deceptive web that, although begun in childhood, was now ready to trap and choke out whatever life and hope was left in me.

Interestingly, in the midst of the dark mess I had created, I continued to play at the top of my "game," working hard, eating little, and sharing my passion for health and fitness all at the same time. Working in the fitness industry fueled my dysfunction beautifully.

I taught eight fitness classes to kids every day then headed off to meet my cardio junkies at the gym for some high flying, old school aerobics that left me drenched and depleted. Sitting down in the shower for fear of fainting became the norm, then onto graduate school before retiring.

I ate just enough to fuel my exercise addiction and enough to keep from being labeled "anorexic." My husband worked nights, which gave me plenty of time to enjoy the "pleasures of adultery" and abuse my body to star in workout videos on the side.

Awarded "Teacher of the Year!" And within 24 hours of receiving the prize money, I rented an apartment and left my husband. In the midst of my silent rage, he continued to ask, "When are we going to have kids?"

"How could you dare bring kids into this lie?!" "How can you pretend things are good, brag about me, and not even know me???" I was convinced these questions justified my defiance.

I never learned to identify my emotions, much less articulate them in order to be known and relieve the pain of feeling invisible. So like many, I found some things to keep me numb.

Desperately seeking answers and waaay past due for some enlightenment, I began the deep work of self-discovery and soon realized the edge I was living on would lead me to glory if I stayed the course and got courageously honest about some things.

I became a tenacious truth seeker and at the age of thirty, life as I knew it came to a screeching halt, and all things became new.

Continual contemplation, journaling, meditation, prayer and Bible study became my new way. A different twelve-step meeting each night, along with writing assignments from my therapist, kept me in a continual state of awareness and intense mindfulness.

Letting go of illusion and fear was difficult. Discovering the faulty belief system driving my life was painful. But my determination to dispel darkness and live under an open heaven was supernatural.

All the emotion I had buried in those silent years began to move through me and break the chains of self-imposed captivity I had always known. It was uncomfortable, but if truth were to set me free, deceit had to flee.

I could feel the sadness of letting go, along with the joy of a new and safe embrace. I rejoiced in the responsibility of choice. My newfound ability to reject fear and choose love inspired and empowered me.

I SHARE MY STORY...

...in the hope of setting you free from the cunning ways of deception. I pray that you might know a life without limitations and live in the love from which you came.

The freedom I've come to know is nothing more than the result of getting honest and renewing my mind to the truth of God's word. Darkness needed to flee, and all emotional ties to the lies had to be severed. In order to live different, I, as well as you, must think, feel and act different.

The most empowering truth I want to leave you with is that your heart holds the beliefs framing your life. They determine your thoughts, words and ways. And until your heart breaks up with fear and unites with love, you will continue to sabotage the deep and true riches of life and intimacy you are designed and destined for.

You hold the thoughts, feelings and intentions of God's heart but choosing to align with them requires serious intention. Divine life and lasting change come only through the working out of the Christ mind within you through hearing and reading and meditating and applying.

Please know that when you choose to live from a divine and infinite mind, deceit and darkness won't stand a chance.

In order to experience real life and lasting change, a letting go of the sensual in exchange for the spiritual must occur. You may need to leave relationships, and the patterns and systems of behavior that no longer serve the divine in you, and embracing the ones that do.

Seeing things from heaven's perspective enables you to make sense out of your experiences and find purpose in and through your pain. As you consume a daily dose of spirit and truth, your thoughts will align with heaven and your words will usher in the abundant life you're here to know.

The voices of defeat, lack and limitation can be overwhelming, but those voices hold only the power you give them. Know that in this one practice of putting off lies and putting on truth, you can expect to see the goodness of God here and now.

Nothing is impossible to the one who believes.

Close your eyes, and see with your spiritual eyes, hear with your spiritual ears, and find the real, true, authentic you. Now let that one arise!

Your start was not about you, but your finish is, and you get to write it! Until your story ends in glory, you're not done.

The gift of redemption is the absolute goodness and grace bestowed upon all those willing to go deep and discover the hindrances that keep them bound to a shallow and sensual life.

You, dear friend, are equipped and empowered to be all and do all. You've got what it takes to overcome and conquer the inevitable obstacles along your way. Make no bones about it, you are graced for your race!

COMPILED BY **ANITA SECHESKY**

Let your ashes be turned to beauty and your mourning to dancing as you pursue, conquer and recover all that's been stolen and know complete restoration of all.

Here's to your greatest triumph, deepest love and brightest tomorrows ~

Much love,
Stacey Cargnelutti

Carol Metz Murray

Carol masterfully uses her voice to inspire women to open to their potential to transform their inner strength into Empowered Leadership. Throughout her life, she had her own journey through anxiety, fear, family strife and out-of-balance living. These experiences led her on a quest to discover and unleash her unique voice.

She is a recognized motivational speaker, and international bestselling author –"Living Without Limitations – 30 Mentors to Rock your World," and "Your Unique Leader's Voice – A Journey Through Trauma," a certified DYBO facilitator, consultant and mentor. She holds a Masters in Public Administration.

As a spiritual entrepreneur Carol has worked with clients regionally, and internationally.

For more information:

www.carolmetzmurray.com

🅢 **carol.metz8.**

🅕 **facebook.com/busempowerment**

🅛 **linkedin.com/pub/carol-metz-murray**

CHAPTER 30

I WAS THAT LITTLE GIRL

By Carol Metz Murray

Imagine yourself as a child, filled with love, laughter and life. The world is your oyster; beauty surrounds you; love and safety are held near and dear without knowing or naming them. As that child you skipped carefree through a meadow totally mesmerized by the sights, sounds, smells. Life is good. Curiosity abounds. Then blackness begins to color the rainbow of curiosity. Laughter silently slips away locked in a time warp. Love feels hollow and life loses its luster. A cloak of painful secrecy veils you, your voice becomes a whisper; and no one comes to help. I remember the debilitating pain, the silence, the humiliation, the aloneness, the fear, the anger and feeling so overwhelmingly unsafe.

I recall asking many questions that remained unanswered:

- Doesn't anyone care about what has just happened to me?
- Why am I all alone in this darkness and silence?
- What must I do to be accepted and loved? and
- Mommy, why am I a "bad" girl; what does it mean that "good girls don't do that?"

This is my story. When I was a little girl I was known as Suzie. At the age of 6 years old I was sexually molested by a neighbor.

What had been a normal, openhearted childhood, turned into a world of fear, confusion, shame, guilt and silence! I tried so hard to talk to my mother, but she couldn't or wouldn't hear me. My young voice was dismissed. I tried so hard to understand what this was all about. What had I done to make this happen to me?

The only one who acknowledged my fear was my Alsatian dog, Rocky. He would growl at this attacker or guard me, keeping him at bay. He was my protector, but unfortunately, Rocky was not always at my side.

I was on my own, living in a trapped world of terror and silence with no one to turn too. Fear and anxiety filled my soul. There was only me to protect me and keep me safe. I dared not get angry, dared not to scream out, good girls didn't do that. I felt so alone and so scared.

The molestations continued for many years. Confusion and guilt filled me. My heart slapped shut. When I was 12, they stopped. But still no one would acknowledge these abominable experiences, much less ask me what lay at the hidden base of the fear, anxiety, stress and emotional void.

When I was 19 I was raped. "There must be something wrong with me," so, as an adult I entered relationships based on what I knew: Silence, Abuse and no Self-Worth.

By 25 I had 4 beautiful babies; and a violence-filled marriage. I knew that if I stayed – I would surely die. Despite my lack of self-worth, and having no one to turn to, I made the move – alone. Step-by-step I began to rebuild my life – along the way unearthing my courage, finding my spirit, and, once again, opening my heart. The strength that I found to leave my marriage helped me raise my children, get work and rise through the ranks until I sustained a respected career and earned my Master's degree.

But the pain filled history of Susie's past wouldn't go away. Just after I turned 40 I hit the wall. It was time to ask for help. But could I or would I ask for help? Who could I trust? I felt like a deflated being. My Soul burst with a tsunami of tears that continued to flood my life day after day, releasing one trapped emotion after another. Through the dense fog I attempted to analyze what had happened, not yet recognizing that after years of abuse my self-worth had been beaten to a pulp. My self-respect was nonexistent. Self-love wasn't even in my vocabulary or on my radar. My health was in tatters. I didn't understand the fierce anger exploding within me like an endless inferno. My dream career had gone up in smoke. How was I to keep my dignity? I felt frustrated that others did not understand. I suffered many losses as my world imploded. I wallowed in fear and anxiety for days on end, attempting to remember my name. I wondered, "Who am I?"

During these depressing times the pain was excruciating and relentless. I felt exposed and isolated; yet denial reigned supreme. Who would listen to me now; no one had before. Past support had been very limited and I had long ago been discouraged by the victim-blaming reactions of others. Their questions suggested they thought there was something "wrong" with me. Who now would really believe that I, who appeared so together on the outside, was tattered and torn and void on the inside? The torture, the fight, the struggle, how could I believe myself or admit that there was really, really anything wrong with me or my life?

I remember, I would hold my head high and say to myself "stand tall, be tall." I had been the independent, self-reliant, strong-willed little girl turned woman who knew how to take care of herself. Trapped inside my blocked emotions, shame consumed me; guilt ate me up; anger poured out of every orifice of my being. There was help everywhere; but did I want it; would I resist it? That would mean opening up, exposing myself, allowing others to see that I was weak, helpless and needy. Wasn't I, why else had all of this happened in my life?

I walked on "eggshells," attempting to contain the fear and anxiety turning inside me. My little girl repeatedly kept calling for comfort, nurturing and love, yes BIG LOVE.

Then one day I recall, as I walked by a wall mirror, when the pain was beyond unbearable and my heart literally felt broken, I heard a tiny, tiny voice deep inside me say "I love you. You are enough. Ask, just reach out and ask for help." Shaken, I peered deep inside my heart to see possibility and the probability of what was yet to be.

At that moment a "Shift" happened; floodgates opened to release encumbered emotions of shame, guilt, fear, anxiety, anger and resentment. In flowed Love. Forgiveness was the sweet spot. My life journey became excruciatingly wonderful with a relentless gentle road of Self-Discovery.

Do you know someone named Suzie who may be in danger or desperately need help? One in Three women in Canada experience physical or sexual violence. If you are in crisis, or know someone who is, or need advice, please call your local emergency help line for free, confidential information. Calling 911 will put you in touch with Emergency services or 211 generally for resources. Check with government and non-government agencies within the community or neighboring community or through schools, colleges and universities for possible services available or for referrals to other resources. It takes tremendous courage to name the pain. And more to decide enough is enough. You can do it.

Whenever people are abused, they do many different things to oppose the abuse and to keep their self-respect and dignity. Sometimes imagining a better life may be the impetus for Courage to stand up and say, "No more." That may be the deciding moment to walk away from it. If you know someone is being abused let them know you are there for them.

The journey of healing is like the alchemist who mines deeply for coal only to discover the alchemy process has turned it into gold. The journey and awareness are priceless. Before 40, I experienced horrific things in my life. Hitting the wall emotionally crippled me. I could not function. There were days I did not know my name. I became unemployed. I was paralyzed with fear and anxiety. Once I worked through the emotional blocks sometimes weeks, sometimes months, sometimes days, I realized that the experiences were not and are not me. What an empowering feeling this was! I am a better, stronger person because of the difficult situations and from having resisted abuse in so many ways.

Sometimes "shift happens" along the way that affects you. It takes courage to step through; it takes support and love, your love to see you through. The lessons I've learned continuously remind me of the greatness I have inside of me. Just like your lessons can remind you. A life experience is not you. A life experience is just that ... an experience that encourages you to mine for your gold. Don't allow it to rule and run your life. Take the experience, mine the Gold. I learned that it is the catalyst to engage, encourage and empower you to step into bigger and greater areas in your life to be YOU. Be open to the possibilities and turn them into probabilities. There is greatness inside of you. I Believe in You.

Inspiration comes from our History and Determines our Future!

Inspiration....only comes when we remember that nothing is determined by the value others place on us. Inspiration comes from the ones in our lives who could have given up so long ago, when others spoke things that could have been our fate.

Inspiration comes from when we see the helpless who have overcome when they had nothing.

Inspiration comes from the wounds that you carry deep inside of you that no one else can see.

Inspiration comes from these wounds that slowly bled for days, months and even years until one day you realized that you and only you could help those wounds to get the help and care they need to truly heal.

Inspiration comes even after losing your first child who had given you dreams to fulfill and plans to make. Inspiration and healing come slowly when you can hear your second baby, a newborn baby boy, cry and coo as you look down into your arms and feel the love of the whole Universe in your grasp; that you are a mother again – and this time you are feeling the emotions in living color. Inspiration comes when God Blesses you again with another beautiful son, your dreams are alive and they are Blessed! God is a good God and he will find ways to Bless you as his child when you least expect it, and in the most amazing and wonderful of ways.

Inspiration comes even after you have been told the most hurtful, degrading and spiteful things you would ever imagine being told to any other human being. You hang your head down for a brief moment and realize that your will to survive is greater and stronger, and when God and your loved ones are on your side, you have nothing to lose.

Inspiration comes when you have a moment of weakness and cannot take the verbal, mental and damaging abuse from people you respect....thoughts of hopelessness and despair flood your intellect and you are on the edge, ready to throw it all away once and for all. Then all of a sudden you have a vision and see that sweet, innocent, beautiful, precious little face looking at you and realize....Life has only just begun!

Inspiration comes to you when you least expect it. When you realize you have a purpose and no matter what anyone has ever said, done or treated you. You really are better than all of that! When you realize that the way people treat one another is really only a reflection of what is going on in their own world, and they are projecting their values and beliefs on you based on their own sad limiting beliefs.

Inspiration comes from the simple pat on the back from a friend or stranger when you have just decided that you cannot do this any longer without confirmation that you're on the right track.

Inspiration comes from the stories of a Grandma who was a widow from the tender age of 28 with 8 children, the oldest being a set of ten year old twins and the two youngest still in diapers, one of whom is your father. Inspiration comes from remembering Grandma only had a grade school education and was given away to live with her future in-laws at the precious age of nine years old. Inspiration comes from hearing how she had no choice but to work after losing my Grandfather, the love of her life.

Inspiration comes in waves when you hear how she had to labor in a rice and cane field with swampy waters and how she was terrified of snakes but had no choice and had to go work. Inspiration comes when I think of how she was offered a second chance at marriage many times and always said no, because of how much she loved her children and did not want her family to be separated. Inspiration comes when I think how my Grandma managed to keep and maintain a large piece of land with fruit and vegetable plantations for her children, all by herself.

Inspiration comes to me and fills my heart once more when I remember this conversation with my late sweet Grandma, "Ma, I feel like I don't fit in." "It doesn't matter if you don't fit in." "I don't fit in." My Grandma told me on her hospital bed, "It doesn't matter if they don't love you! I love you and Jesus Loves you." My beloved Grandma whispered to me through her pain....Oh how I wish I had crawled into her hospital bed and held her close, like she did to me as a child. But I had just finished working and still had on my scrubs and did not want to soil her bed. It was the last time she told me those words before she passed, to be reunited with the love of her life, my Grandfather, who had passed so many years before. I will never forget her love and words of inspiration to me and all of her loved ones over the years.

Inspiration comes from having a mom who was raised by a step-mother who was abusive and neglectful, and by a father who was absent and an alcoholic. Inspiration comes from hearing your own story of how your mom's pregnancy with you was almost terminated so many times and she had to have blood transfusions and be hospitalized to carry you to full term.

Inspiration comes from hearing the story of being a toddler and your parents were told that, as a young child with gastroenteritis in South America, your chances of survival were next to none, even after being seen and treated by four pediatricians and doctors, and they had given up, informing my parents they should be planning a service. But then understanding that your young parents who loved you so much decided to take turns reading the Bible out loud all night over you while you were sleeping, and through their faith and dedication you survived and amazed the doctors.

Inspiration comes and changes everything; it can and will change your destiny if you let it! It can be when a stranger believes in you, and God and the Universe set it up and all that was once negative and discouraging and damaging has now been replaced by all that is positive, encouraging and beautiful!

There is hope for all that are hopeless! There is strength for the weak! There is love for the unloved and there is a place in the heart of those who are compassionate and full of mercy and grace for those who are in need.

Inspiration comes from life, all around us. Yes, when I hear the things others have gone through I realize I have a lot to be "Thankful for," and recognize it's time to give back! Inspiration is all around us. Are you looking? Are you appreciating? Are you grateful?

Inspiration comes from looking past your current situation and seeing what else is out there and how much others need your seeds of hope and to know and understand their own value.

Inspiration is the foundation of a Life without Limitations.

These are bits and pieces of my life story, what is yours?

We all have one; check yours and see where you were and where you are now. The future never looked Brighter!

God Bless each and every one of you!

Love
Anita Sechesky

Afterthought

So now that you have read each of these Powerful and Inspirational Chapters, and understand what each of my wonderful co-authors have contributed to make my Vision for this book come to pass, I trust you can now appreciate how I was intent on making your healing become the center of our focus.

I want to encourage you, my dear reader, to stretch and let go of your own personal limitations as you continue to ponder the wisdom and experiences of these co-authors. They have openly allowed you into their worlds of pain and heartache.

As you can see, these individuals are accessible and real people just like you and me. Please feel free to reach out and connect with whomever you choose to.

The value that is within this book is priceless. Just like Gold never loses its value, the knowledge these lives poured into their Chapters is priceless and worthy of review and application in one's daily life.

Now, my question to you is, what does your life look like? Are you struggling with keeping your own life issues, business or family together? Have you wondered what it could be like to finally accomplish the things you have been dreaming of for so long?

As you can see, I have "Successfully" managed, mentored, consulted, and organized two international groups of co-authors in less than one year! That's approximately 60 people from around the world!

I would love to help you to organize and manage your business goals, just like I have done for myself! This is what I enjoy most about empowering individuals or groups of people so they can reach their goals in as short a time possible and then see their productive results! I have learned through experience and my extensive training (as a Level 3 – Advanced Certified Life Coach, NLP Practitioner, Law of Attraction Wealth Practitioner and Registered Nurse) how people cope effectively by having an organized system that brings balance with positive results! There really is a secret to helping others succeed just for you! I want to show you how.

It is not always easy to keep it together – whether a company, business or people – and also have things running smoothly while building the life of your dreams.

I understand the frustrations, tears and stress. I want to assist you in making your dreams and goals a reality.

Together we can develop a "Master Plan for Your Own Success" and along the way eliminate any "Limiting Beliefs" that have been stopping you all this time. You may even be surprised at what you discover! Your passion is where your strength is. My passion is all about bringing your passion to life.

Let's do this! Connect with me and let me mentor and coach you on how you can step into "Living Your Life Without Limitations!"

asechesky@hotmail.ca

With much Love and Appreciation,
Anita Sechesky

The End

CPSIA information can be obtained at www.ICGtesting.com
Printed in the USA
LVOW10s1534130414

381508LV00015B/1006/P